Marketing Your Consulting and Professional Services

THIRD EDITION

Marketing Your Consulting and Professional Services

Dick Connor, CMC   Jeff Davidson, CMC

John Wiley & Sons, Inc.

New York • Chichester • Weinheim • Brisbane • Singapore • Toronto

This text is printed on acid-free paper.

Copyright © 1997 by Richard A. Connor, Jr., and Jeffrey P. Davidson.
Published by John Wiley & Sons, Inc.

All rights reserved. Published simultaneously in Canada.

This publication is designed to provide accurate and authoritative
information in regard to the subject matter covered. It is sold with
the understanding that the publisher is not engaged in rendering legal,
accounting, or other professional services. If legal advice or other expert
assistance is required, the services of a competent professional person
should be sought.

Library of Congress Cataloging-in-Publication Data:

Connor, Richard A.
    Marketing your consulting and professional services / Dick Connor,
Jeffrey P. Davidson.—3rd ed.
        p.   cm.
    Rev. ed. of: Marketing your consulting and professional services.
    Includes index.
    ISBN 0-471-13392-2 (cloth : alk. paper)
        1. Professions—Marketing—Handbooks, manuals, etc.
    2. Consultants—Marketing—Handbooks, manuals, etc.   I. Davidson,
Jeffrey P.   II. Connor, Richard A.   Marketing your consulting and
professional services.   III. Title.
    HD69.C6C63   1997
    658.8—dc21   97-22965
                                                                CIP

Printed in the United States of America

10   9   8   7   6   5   4   3   2   1

Introduction

Although the technology right in your own office enables you to contact thousands of prospects, when it comes to *Marketing Your Consulting and Professional Services*, today's reality is that you don't get rich trying to be everything to everyone. Your goal is to sense, serve, and highly satisfy carefully targeted clients in ways that encourage them to use even more of your services and sing your praises to others.

This third edition *had* to be written because the world is changing at warp speed. Always on the heels of change comes opportunity, especially if you take the time to analyze the dynamics of what your clients and prospects face. Increasingly, the target markets you wish to serve are forced to do more with less, and hence strive to reduce costs. Happily, that means many clients are relying on outsourcing of services, perhaps services that you can readily provide.

There is unrelenting pressure on organizations of all sizes to produce profits. Markets are being driven by forces and factors that end up creating a different type of client than you used to serve. The computer revolution, changing demographics patterns, TQM (Total Quality Management), and re-engineering, among many other factors, are irrevocably changing the form and structure of countless organizations. Information technology, LANs (local area networks), imaging, CD-ROMs, virtual organizations, and telecommuting are impacting all major industries. Information is becoming democratized and shared between new variations of strategic partnerships. Concurrently, there is an intense focus on customers, continuing process improvement is sought, and downsizing is taking its toll.

The key to market survival in virtually all professions is to obtain accurate, critical information faster, and then to mine this information both for the knowledge it is capable of producing and for subsequent opportunities that emerge. Powerful desktop PCs now enable even the smallest professional services firm to launch a highly targeted marketing and new client development campaign. Rather than having to compete on a level playing field, *the client-centered marketer can transform the target market into a slippery slope for the competition.*

The marketing challenge you face today is far different than what you faced even as recently as 10 years ago. The task has changed from marketing and selling one's services to promoting and providing solutions that clients regard as worthy and valuable to them, particularly promising solutions that clients regard as "hot-button" issues and debilitating problems. Make no mistake: The changes and challenges that professional service marketers face today are as profound as the difference between chess and checkers. In short, both the play and the strategy are distinctive and more complex. Satisfying high-potential clients for their long-term client retention, for example, has replaced landing new clients as the driving force among successful service providers. Also, the best firms are developing a keener strategic business focus while ensuring that the execution and delivery of their services are uniformly excellent.

What will you learn from this book that will make a significant impact in your business and life?

1. *How to make the most of your relationships.* The book will show you how to make the most from your current and future relationships by teaching you leveraging techniques that just are not available on this level anywhere.

2. *How to make Client-Centered Marketing™ a natural activity.* Because you'll develop a client-centered focus, you'll always have the needs and concerns of clients uppermost in your mind; hence, marketing will become a natural activity.

3. *How to work from your comfort zone.* You'll work where you're most comfortable, because there will be dozens of reminders throughout the book on how to stay comfortable and at ease with marketing your services.

4. *How to ensure satisfaction.* Most importantly, you will become a master in ensuring satisfaction, which, in itself, will become the benchmark of successful professionals for years to come. It's the one skill and capability that will never become outdated.

This third edition has been restructured and rewritten to reflect the changes and forces you face in marketing your services and ensuring client satisfaction. While built on the foundation of the earlier editions, this edition contains 14 completely new chapters, and every existing chapter has been updated and rewritten. Words are spared in this edition, offering the essence of what you need without bogging you down. There are more precise definitions of terminology to help you avoid misunderstandings and to help cultivate a client-centered focus as you read.

Books are linear information vehicles and so is this one. To help you move about the book more freely, we've inserted linkage points in each chapter that will enable you more readily to engage in parallel activities. Also included, in Appendix B, is a variety of the best resources to ensure your profitability, including specific addresses and contact information. We unabashedly recommend our own resources and learning aids, since we know that they will give you the edge in your market. Our focus is on ensuring that you receive the very best advice and instruction in marketing your services.

Acknowledgments

DICK CONNOR'S ACKNOWLEDGMENTS

Jeff Davidson, my coauthor, who got the entire process rolling.

Sam Beachem, my mentor at Booz Allen, who taught me how to think and write like a consultant.

Joel Goldsmith, whose words of wisdom guide my days.

Werner, for a gift that keeps on giving.

Peter Drucker, management thinker and author whose insights triggered the development of the client-centered marketing approach.

Susan, my wife and best friend, who is always there for me.

JEFF DAVIDSON'S ACKNOWLEDGMENTS

Dick Connor, my coauthor and the father of client-centered marketing.

Robert Fritz, for a world of personal insights that keep unfolding.

Tony Alessandra, a pal and mentor par excellence.

Valerie Davidson, my best office worker and daily inspiration.

DICK AND JEFF'S ACKNOWLEDGMENTS

Our wonderful clients everywhere, for their enthusiasm, diligence, and loyalty.

Mike Hamilton, our editor, for his guidance in getting the third edition published, Linda Witzling and Monika Jain for their able assistance, Lauren Fransen, for selling this book all over the world, Peter Clifford, for making bright lights shine on it, and Dr. Stephen Kippur, for opening the door 12 years ago.

Thanks to Ed Becker, Ron Wagner, Craig Gibson, and Dheeraj Vasishta, who reviewed and improved our text, to Megan P. Boyle for ace proofreading of the galleys, and to Missy Garnett at Cape Cod Compositors, who worked magic in producing the final product.

Contents

This section focuses on your targets of opportunity and targets of attention. Targets represent the relationships and marketing factors that need your attention and, often, your action. Your goal in managing this element is to efficiently replenish and expand your desired target niche. Clients and others in this element represent your potential new business opportunities.

Developing an insider's understanding of the niche involves getting client-smart about the working of the client's industry and market.

This section discusses the importance of strategic
thinking, presents the authors' personal strategic
plans, and summarizes key client-centered points.

List of Figures

PART ONE

Foundational Material

CHAPTER 1

The Client-Centered Marketing Process

This chapter introduces you to the client-centered marketing (CCM) process originated in 1972 by Dick Connor. Thousands of successful service marketers in several dozen nations in virtually every size and type of professional practice or service business use CCM. It works for them, and it can work for you, too.

It is our belief, based on extensive consulting experience with service providers worldwide, that to ensure both your survival and your profitable growth in the 1990s and beyond, CCM needs to be the driving force behind your entire service firm. We make this statement because our "in-the-trenches" experience shows that the four core components of the CCM system—(1) client focus, (2) value-adding solutions, (3) client satisfaction, and (4) niche-specific, insider's knowledge—will *always* be your source of competitive advantage and high-margin revenue.

After completing this chapter and absorbing the ideas presented, you will be able to:

☐ Define client-centered marketing for yourself and enlist others in creating and participating in such a program.

☐ Identify marketing objectives that can be achieved through your client-centered marketing program.

☐ Define *leveraging* in your own terms and recognize the impact it can have in your situation.

☐ Relate the notion of your marketing comfort zone to your situation.

☐ Answer the question, "What is value to the client?"

☐ Avoid making typical marketing mistakes.

INTRODUCING CLIENT-CENTERED MARKETING

Client-centered marketing is a core business process that makes an individual client or high-potential prospect in a targeted industry–market niche the focus and beneficiary of your specialized niche information, resources, and experience. The strategic decision to employ client-centered marketing encompasses:

1. Selecting a targeted industry–market niche for special attention.

2. Developing an insider's understanding of the industry and market as a means of identifying current and emerging hot-button needs you can meet with resources available to you.

3. Preparing, positioning, promoting, and providing value-adding solutions to selected hot-button needs of clients and high-potential prospects in the niche.

4. Leveraging the time, resources, and relationships available to you.

CCM involves developing a superior, continuing relationship with your most desirable clients within a niche. Once this special relationship is established, the primary and continuing task of the client-centered marketer is to *sense, sell, serve,* and *satisfy* the hot-button needs and expectations of all involved in the recommendation, purchase, installation, and use of what we call value-adding solutions.

A WORKING DEFINITION

Before we go further, let's look at a number of terms used in the preceding paragraphs. Each of these will be defined here and included in the Glossary found at the back of the book.

A *client* is an individual or organization you have served or are now serving. Please note that our use of the term *client* throughout the book refers to customers, accounts, patients, or others whom you have billed for products or services that you provided. Your clients represent your current sources of revenue.

A *prospect* is a potential client. This could be an organization or an individual. A prospect is a party who has agreed to discuss a hot-button need situation with you. (A *suspect* is a desirable nonclient organization or individual possessing suspected needs for your services whom you have yet to contact.)

A *strategic* decision sets the direction of your business. Choosing an industry–market niche for concentration, a strategic decision, is one of the most important moves you will make regarding the long-term viability of your practice.

The term *industry* refers to your clients and prospects who are sellers or providers of similar goods and services. Hence, they may market to the same type of prospects. For example, Dick serves clients in the accounting profession, the U.S. federal government, and management and marketing consultants. Jeff serves associations in the financial services industry such as banking, financial planning, and real estate; health services administrators, doctors, nurses, and support staff; and corporations including top executives, mid-level management, and supervisory staff.

Market refers to your industry-specific clients and prospects who are current and potential buyers for your services. A market refers to the postal ZIPs and cyberspace—the Web sites and Usenet groups—in which you promote and provide your service solutions.

Niche is shorthand for an industry–market niche, and is comprised of clients and prospects in the same industry who can be reached and served in your market.

A *hot-button need* is any topic, issue, problem, opportunity, or trend that is of keen interest to the client or prospect whom you are seeking to serve.

Value-adding solutions satisfy the hot-button need, meet or exceed the expectations of those involved in the purchase and use of the solution, and enhance a client's competitive advantage by either lowering cost, increasing revenue, or improving performance/productivity. We have taken the popular notion of providing value-added services a step further then by including the level of quality you build into the solution as part of the value you have added. As such, a value-adding solution is the gift that keeps on giving once it has been installed in the client's environment.

A SIX-PART PLAN

There are six client-centered marketing activities that when incorporated in your business will give you a decided competitive edge over others in your industry or profession. These are:

1. Selecting a targeted industry–market niche for special attention.
2. Developing an insider's understanding of the niche's industry and markets.
3. Building a favorable awareness and earning an insider's reputation with targeted members of the niche.
4. Preparing, positioning, promoting, and providing value-adding solutions to hot-button needs.
5. Building superior, value-based relationships with all who are or can be influential to you in meeting your marketing goals.
6. Leveraging your knowledge, experience, and resources.

Let's visit each activity, in sequence.

Selecting a Targeted Industry–Market Niche

Markets are in a constant state of flux, client expectations are ever-changing, and the world economy keeps dramatically evolving. You can't be all things to all people, and you certainly can't be all things to all clients. The core success factor today is directing your resources and attention to niches that you can easily penetrate and where you can most readily serve prosperously. *Sometimes it takes intestinal fortitude to resist diverting resources and attention to some niches potentially lucrative to you, and concentrate on those that you can more easily penetrate and more readily serve.*

Building an Insider's Understanding of the Niche

Insider's understanding refers to your in-depth knowledge of the structure and dynamics of the industry and market—how the niche works, what it takes to make a profit and compete successfully, the key players you know and need to know, and the buying process of your clients and prospects. If you lack in-depth knowledge of the structure and dynamics of the industry and market, or there are gaping holes in your knowledge as to how the niche works and what it takes to make a profit, your critical task becomes building your insider's understanding of the niche.

Earning an Insider's Reputation

It's one thing to build an insider's understanding of the niche. It's quite another to develop an *insider's reputation*—the favorable awareness of you and your business by clients, prospects, and others who appreciate your niche-specific expertise. When working properly, your insider's reputation opens doors to new clients, gets you favorable mention in the media, and engenders invitations to join and serve in prestigious organizations serving the niche.

Providing Value-Adding Solutions to Hot-Button Needs

Preparing, positioning, promoting, and providing value-adding solutions to hot-button needs gives you a competitive edge. Clients want a more favorable or assured future and are willing to pay for it. Once clients understand and approve of your value-adding solutions, you've laid the groundwork for additional business.

Building Superior Value-Based Relationships

Value-based relationships develop as a result of your understanding of the niche, and your experience and resources for meeting the needs and expectations of your clients, prospects, and niche influentials. A value-based relationship is often called a win-win relationship. Building a win-win relationship requires that you invest your time and attention with the client, provide client-centered information and service, and, often, provide plain old hand-holding.

Leveraging Your Knowledge, Experience, and Resources

The notion of *leveraging* is integral to effective client-centered marketing. One dictionary defines leverage as "the advantage or gained power from an action." We define leveraging as concentrating the smallest amount of your resources on the fewest clients and prospects that will disproportionately produce the largest amount of profit and results.

NOT FOR EVERY CLIENT AT FIRST

If you're thinking that you don't want to expend this type of effort on everyone, relax. A client-centered marketing and client service approach will probably not be appropriate for all your current clients.

Rather, it is reserved for the approximately 20 percent of your clients with a high potential for needing additional services from you. Thereafter, your client-centered marketing goal is to increase the level of service and satisfaction to an increasing number of high-potential clients in high-potential niches.

We suggest that you serve the remaining 80 percent of your other acceptable clients in a business-as-usual manner. Any clients that you deem to be unacceptable at this time will need to be upgraded to acceptable (more on this in later chapters) or replaced. Since you are a busy service provider who struggles often daily with finding and allocating time for new business development, we advise that you leverage your time, talents, and technology.

BENEFITS OF CLIENT-CENTERED MARKETING

Okay, so if you buy into the plan we're going to present to you, what do you get? In a nutshell, you'll be able to grow your business without having to engage in aggressive prospecting and personal selling.

Prospecting is the process of identifying and contacting high-potential organizations and individual businesspeople in your markets ("suspects"). Ultimately, you want to get appointments with them to discuss your proposed solutions to what you've come to understand as their problem(s). Please note: Once a "suspect" agrees to meet with you the suspect becomes a prospect.

Personal selling refers to the face-to-face discussion with a client or prospect regarding a hot-button need for which you propose to deliver a solution. How much more relaxed and effective you'll be when you don't have to engage in aggressive personal selling to market your consulting or professional services.

A second primary benefit of client-centered marketing is that you'll be able to market and serve clients from your current marketing comfort zone. What's a comfort zone? Frequently, when speaking to clients or other groups, Dick mentions that he is a scuba diver. His current comfort zone when diving is in the 60-to-70-foot range. Diving at this depth, he is alert and relaxed, enjoying himself while not being preoccupied with surviving the dive. Beyond, say, 75 or 80 feet, Dick's experience of scuba diving changes—it's not so much fun.

Your current *marketing comfort zone* refers to the marketing, client service, and new business development activities in which you have confidence. It is where you are proactive and productive in your communications and actions. Not surprisingly, a large portion of your current marketing comfort zone is dependent upon the industry-specific knowledge, skills, and attitudes you have acquired by serving your best clients in a niche.

The value in using the client-centered marketing approach is that you work primarily in your current comfort zone. This is in direct contrast to other approaches that involve pitching your services to disinterested people who wish you would go away, display outright resistance, and make you feel rejected and dejected.

CLIENT-CENTERED MARKETING VERSUS OTHER MARKETING APPROACHES

To understand why we advocate a client-centered marketing approach it may be helpful to contrast it with other approaches to marketing currently in use.

The *marketing-driven* approach is based on advertising, heavy promotion, and emphasis on image development. Firms following this approach focus on getting known in the community or region as providers of good products and services at reasonable prices. However, in addition to costly and time-consuming self-promotion, this approach also requires the development of aggressive personal selling skills.

The *market-driven* approach has a subtle word difference with the approach above. This approach focuses on building relationships with key players in the market and developing an understanding of the general needs of the market. However, by not taking the analysis to the individual client level as in the client-centered marketing approach, firms practicing a market-driven approach often find themselves losing out to more client-centered competitors, without knowing why.

The *traditional marketing* approach is reactive, to say the least. Growth is assumed to be the result of providing good products or services to meet the general needs of the marketplace. Generally, the service provider misses opportunities to be of service because of failure to be attuned to recognizing them. Also, the service provider learns about problems only when they are brought forward by an upset client or prospect. Today, waiting for someone to seek your assistance is risky.

Service providers using the *hard-sell* approach put emphasis on communicating about their firm, their products and services, and their people. They assume that growth is largely the result of being known, instead of focusing on providing solutions to the hot-button needs of their high-potential clients and prospective clients. Increasingly, clients and prospective clients dislike the hard sell. Subtly or obviously, clients will make it harder for you to see them if you employ a hard-sell approach.

CLIENT-CENTERED MARKETING IN PERSPECTIVE

Our experience in working with service marketers in many niches indicates that without major program status, marketing is seldom effective and long-lasting. A successful business or practice can be compared with a balanced four-legged stool:

Leg 1 is technical quality: consistent, superb service and technology delivered on a timely basis. This is the value-added component talked about today by many marketers.

Leg 2 is engagement administration: billing for work done, invoicing in ways that show all of your billed and unbilled actions, and collecting fees on a timely basis.

Leg 3 is resource development: acquiring and developing the people, tools, and revenues required for providing value-adding solutions.

Leg 4 is client-centered marketing: making an individual client or prospect, in a targeted industry–market niche, the beneficiary of your niche-specific service(s).

INSIGHTS AND LESSONS LEARNED

The essence of client-centered marketing is *the development of superior relationships based on technical and personal factors that create a high degree of interdependence.* Professionals who are effective in marketing have learned along the way to develop relationships with clients and others who are willing and able to assist them in their various marketing and selling activities.

Here are some provocative thoughts for you to carry into the next chapter:

1. Value is always defined by the recipient, not the provider. Value is in the eyes and emotions of receivers, and is always rooted in their personal and organizational needs systems, and their experience with your type of service. Value is a function of needs being identified and satisfied in ways that meet and/or exceed expectations.

2. Clients don't purchase your services and products; they buy your promise to work with them in creating a more favorable future, as

they define it. Your promise includes one or more deliverables and ancillary actions such as training, all delivered within a network of value-based relationships.

3. Services are really bought or rejected in the gut by clients. They then justify the buy/no-buy decision to themselves and others by the use of hard copy, such as competitive proposals and testimonials from others who support their decision.

Taking a consistent CCM approach to developing new business will assist you in achieving the following marketing objectives:

1. Generating controlled, profitable growth.
2. Expanding services to current clients.
3. Retaining desirable clients.
4. Attracting desirable prospects.
5. Capitalizing on the potential within your business/practice.
6. Managing your image with clients and targets.

Each of these objectives will be covered in detail in later chapters.

Having introduced client-centered marketing, we turn now to a detailed discussion of the client-centered marketing process model.

CHAPTER 2

The Client-Centered Marketing Process Model

This chapter presents our model of the client-centered marketing process. In its simplest terms, a process pulls together inputs to produce outputs that deliver value. The client-centered marketing process is a set of activities designed to produce and deliver value to your market targets. For example, a baseball team practices during spring training with the hope of fielding a unified team that wins games and thus attracts loyal fans who are more than willing to repeatedly pay high-ticket prices. An auto manufacturer continually retools to ensure that the type of high-quality cars customers want can be assembled in a cost-effective, speedy manner.

> The core and continuing purpose of the client-centered marketing process is to help you leverage your activities to ensure the satisfaction and long-term retention of key clients.

There are four elements in the model of the client-centered marketing process, including:

1. Current business/profession factors.
2. Leverage relationships.
3. Targets.
4. Value-adding factors.

Each element and its related marketing and sales factors impacts your current ability to provide client service, while simultaneously imposing limits on your potential for growth. As such, you'll need to continually manage the marketing and sales factors of each element.

After you carefully examine the four elements you'll be better able to:

☐ Trace the flow of marketing information critical to your success and take effective action to secure any type of information you're not currently receiving.

☐ Identify other key factors that require your attention.

☐ Apply the principle of leveraging to your key clients.

☐ Be more effective in making contact with prospects.

☐ Work within your marketing comfort zone.

Figure 2–1 shows the content and flow of information for each of the four elements and their relationship to each other.

CURRENT BUSINESS/PROFESSION FACTORS

There are six factors in this element:

1. *Financial performance*—your most recent three- to five-year personal financial performance expressed in terms of hours billed, total revenue, and percentage of change.

2. *Clients* you are now serving, or will serve during the current marketing period, expressed by the percentage of total fees they represent and their potential for additional services.

3. *Industries/professions* in which you now serve clients and seek prospects, expressed by percentage of total fees they represent and the potential for growth.

4. *Markets* in which you serve clients and seek prospects, expressed by the percentage of total fees they represent and their potential for growth.

5. *Services* you promote and provide to clients, expressed as percentage of total fees for the marketing period under study, along with an assessment of their technology and potential for generating additional revenue.

FIGURE 2–1
Client-Centered Marketing Process Model

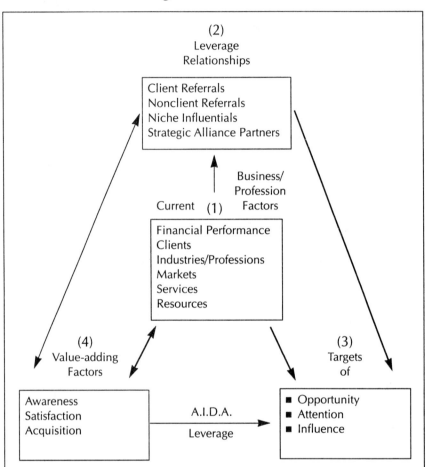

Copyright © 1997 by Dick Connor, CMC

6. *Resources*—money, skills, technology, and information that are available to you in marketing your solutions.

LEVERAGE RELATIONSHIPS

Leverage relationships assist you in developing new business. The four classes of leverage relationships are:

1. *Client referrals.* Clients who are especially satisfied with your services and relationships will often provide you with leads and introductions to prospects, give you written testimonials, speak well of you to their colleagues, and seek to involve you in their professional and trade association activities.

2. *Nonclient referrals.* Attorneys, bankers, and others in your market who are respected by your clients and prospects are valuable referral sources.

3. *Niche influentials (NIs).* Key players in the niche's industry and market; NIs include industry and market analysts, competitors, gurus, and editors of publications that are read by and influence clients and prospects.

4. *Strategic alliance partners.* The relationships you have with other individuals and organizations serving the niche can assist you in preparing, promoting, and providing value-adding solutions.

When undertaking new business development activities, such as identifying targets of opportunity, most people find that they are effective when calling on clones of their current, better clients. As used here, working from your comfort zone means calling on prospects and suspects with whom you have some type of affinity. You feel comfortable calling on them, and you can speak their business language. Any anxieties you may feel remain at an acceptable level. As discussed in Chapter 1, working from your comfort zone enables you to assume effective self-initiated marketing behavior.

Of the four major elements in the client-centered marketing system, current business/profession factors and leverage relationships form the bedrock of your current practice. These first two elements largely define where you live and work, and where you generate your current and short-term fees. Both elements are already a part of your marketing comfort zone—the range of activities and relationships in which you can comfortably and confidently interact with clients and people with whom you have a leverage relationship.

TARGETS

Targets include existing clients with additional needs, all prospects, and additional leverage relationships that you seek to develop. The goal of targeting is to enable you to leverage your time by identifying individuals and organizations that warrant your special attention. Targets represent your leverage opportunities. Targets enable you to market on a bits-and-pieces basis, which is ideal for the busy marketer. The 80/20 rule holds here as elsewhere; a moderate amount of any factor tends to produce a disproportionate share of results.

When you boil it all down, there are three basic target categories:

1. *Targets of opportunity* include all current high-potential clients, prospects and suspects in your new-business pipeline, all active referral sources, targeted industry-market niches needing to be cultivated and developed, and potential strategic alliance partners with whom you wish to develop a relationship.

2. *Targets of attention* refer to all important relationships, programs, services, systems, and resources that require monitoring and/or corrective action during the current marketing period.

3. *Targets of influence* are the additional niche influentials with whom you wish to develop a relationship.

VALUE-ADDING FACTORS

There are three client-centered marketing processes that require your focused time and attention. A client-centered marketing process is a set of activities designed to produce and deliver value to your market targets. The three processes form the link between your clients or targets and the firm.

1. *Awareness.* This core marketing process includes several subprocesses:

   Positioning is the marketing strategy of designing and presenting the intended image of your business and communicating the benefits of your services so they occupy a distinctive and valued place in the minds and emotions of your targets of opportunity and niche influentials.

   Designing your intended image is a way of differentiating your business and solutions from others and identifying the important value you are able to deliver.

   Promotion refers to the process of informing, persuading, or reminding targets of opportunity and targets of influence about your firm's ability to meet selected needs in the niche. This process includes earning an insider's reputation through your speaking engagements, writing effective, client-centered publications, and leveraging memberships by joining and serving with distinction in important niche organizations.

2. *Satisfaction*. This process involves managing and shaping client expectations, and delivering and installing the solution that exceeds expectations of all involved in the purchase and use of the solution.

3. *Acquisition*. This process is dedicated to developing new revenue from clients and high-potential prospects who become new clients. New revenue is developed by providing additional services to clients, and billing and collecting more. New clients are acquired by prospecting, personal selling, and stimulating inquiries from clients and prospects. Acquisition is comprised of several subprocesses, including:

   Prospecting involves finding qualified suspects and then contacting them to obtain appointments to discuss one or more of their needs.

   Personal selling refers to the face-to-face new business discussions you plan for and conduct with your clients and prospects.

THE AIDA PROCESS

In addition to elements 1 through 4 of the client-centered marketing process model (Figure 2–1), notice the letters "A.I.D.A." What do these mean? The AIDA process involves creating a favorable awareness (A), sharing information (I) to develop a client's or prospect's interest in seeing you, conducting need-driven discussions (D), and building a desire to proceed to action (A).

The AIDA process has traditionally been used by multinational manufacturers and distributors in product marketing to describe the phases involved in the capture of a new customer. However, the model lends itself well to adaptation for your services marketing as well. The model has four phases that you have to plan for and execute if your new business development activities are to be effective:

1. The first "A" represents the goal of obtaining the attention and favorable awareness of targets of opportunity and targets of influence.

2. The "I" represents information that you send to targets. This information is designed to interest targets so that they agree to

meet with you after you have successfully completed a telephone contact.

3. The "D" represents new business discussions with members of the decision-making unit in the targeted organization. These new business discussions are designed to define the gap between what currently is and what is desired or required by the prospective client. Showing how your proposed solution will decrease the deviation between what currently is and what is desired by the prospective client is at the heart of the new business discussion.

4. The second "A" represents the agreed-upon actions you and the prospective client will take to meet a mutually defined need. Actions may include the preparation and presentation of a proposal or undertaking a survey where the client allows you to interview additional key people.

As you proceed through the book, much of what has been discussed so far will come to you more easily. For now, simply recognize that when you examine the individual components leading to new business development, you see that promotion involves obtaining attention and awareness and generating interest in response to information (AI). Prospecting involves generating interest and obtaining appointments for new business discussions (ID). Personal selling contacts involve managing the discussions with contacts and moving toward agreed-upon actions (DA).

Now that you've completed the essential background information, let's turn to Part Two, Marketing Factors Analysis.

Marketing Factors Analysis

CHAPTER 3

Preparing for a Marketing Analysis of Your Current Business or Practice

In his book *Managing for Results*, Dr. Peter Drucker says, "Knowledge, organized in a discipline, does a good deal for the merely competent; it endows him with some effectiveness. It does infinitely more for the truly able; it endows him with excellence." This chapter presents the procedures analyzing the key marketing factors that drive your business. The importance of this preparation cannot be overstated. Your goal is to select the most relevant data—with your personal computer (PC), if possible—to convert this into knowledge that can then be organized and further leveraged.

After reading this chapter and absorbing the ideas, you will be able to:

- ☐ Select a marketing information system (MIS) software program that is right for you.

- ☐ Determine essential data to be accumulated.

- ☐ Explore the use of data entry forms.

- ☐ Review a set of reports and lists used in subsequent analysis.

SELECTING YOUR MIS SOFTWARE PROGRAM

Selecting a software program for your marketing information system (MIS) is a strategic decision. You know too well from other software you've used that once you begin using one program, switching to a new software program is seldom easy to do and can be costly in many respects.

In Chapter 18 you'll learn how to build the complete MIS, which consists of databases, a niche-specific library, and your marketing and engagement tools. To manage the data you already have and the data you will be collecting, and to capitalize on the information contained in the library you will be assembling, you will need to choose an appropriate database software package. This software needs to be multifunctional, yet easy to learn and use. Specifically, the program must enable you to:

1. Enter an ever-increasing amount of both structured and unstructured data, as well as graphic images from a variety of sources and in many different forms.

2. Find data or information when you need it and present it in a manner of your choice.

3. Prepare attractive hard-copy deliverables such as marketing reports, merged mail promotional letters, proposals, and engagement letters.

We recommend using askSam, a database management program that feels like the word processor program you probably are using currently. We've used a variety of database programs, but askSam is the easiest to use and has the most features that will help you win more clients and keep your marketing costs at a minimum. You can reach the company in a variety of ways:

For More Information about askSam

Tel.: 800-800-1997 (sales), 904-584-6590   Fax: 904-584-7481
E-mail: info@asksam.com   http://www.asksam.com

You may also want to consult a database expert to assist you in making this strategic choice. If you use CompuServe, click into the Office Automation Forum for a discussion about the advantages of personal information managers (PIMs), contact managers, and sales automation programs.

PREPARING FOR DATA ENTRY

Your goal in data entry is to be able to enter data once and then, at your convenience, leverage it many times, in many ways. Careful preparation is the watchword in this step: "Good data in leads to good information out." We ask that you prepare the following lists of key marketing factors information.

1. Prepare a list of current clients served during the most recent 12-month period.

   - Rank these clients in descending order of revenues obtained from them during the most recent 12 months.

   - If you serve several clients in the same industry belonging to a parent company whom you also serve, group the revenues and consider them as one.

2. Prepare a list of current prospects you are attempting to convert into new clients. Rank them in descending order of revenues expected to be obtained from them during the next 12-month period. Make educated guesses if you have to.

3. Develop an "Industries Served" list. Your goal is to have a readily available list of industries in which you serve and seek clients to be used as you complete three data entry forms discussed later in the chapter (Figures 3–1, 3–2, and 3–3).

   - Refer to Appendix A, which presents Standard Industrial Classification (SIC) categories. This is an industry list for consistently classifying and referring to various industries in both the government and private sectors. To conserve space, Appendix A offers an abbreviated list containing the most popular codes.

   - If you serve clients whose industry is not included in Appendix A, we suggest that you contact American Business Information for a free copy of their "Lists of 10 Million Businesses." They offer an alternative and voluminous list of SIC information and names. They can be reached at: http://www.abii.com or write to:

American Business Information
5711 South 86th Circle
P.O. Box 27347
Omaha, NE 68127

- Other list providers can be found in the yellow pages of your local telephone directory. Review your list of current clients, and determine the industry in which each operates. List the industries by written description and four-digit SIC number.

- Alphabetize the industry descriptions to make them easier to find.

4. Develop a "Services Provided" list. Review the services you provide to develop major categories of services offered.

Examples from Successful Firms

Here are the ways two of our clients categorized their services in accordance with the procedure outlined above:

Craig Gibson, vice president of marketing for Cambridge Transnational Associates, Inc., an international trade firm, views his market offerings:

International network development.
International development counseling.
Foreign patent referral-building.

Ed Becker, vice president of Virginia-based Signal Corp, sees his major service offerings as:

Information technology.
Computer-integrated systems design.
Computer programming services.

Please don't shortcut this step. You'll be tracking the revenue produced by each major service category during the life of your business. So, it's critical that you carefully think through your selection of your major service categories.

PREPARING YOUR DATA ENTRY FORMS

Each of the three forms has been carefully developed and tested with clients of all sizes of businesses. Hence, you don't need to add additional fields unless you see a special need for the additional data. Besides, your goal here is simplicity—you'll be developing a set of more complete data entry forms in later chapters.

Current Client Data Entry

Figure 3–1 is the Current Client Data Entry Form. There are seven fields into which you will enter structured data. Three of the fields—industry, market, and services—are amenable to using a picklist. A picklist or dropdown list is a predefined list of entries for a field. For example, instead of typing the name of a service, you develop a service picklist which enables you to click the appropriate name to enter the description. If you use askSam, or are able to program this feature on your software, you'll appreciate the speed and accuracy of your data entry.

To complete the client data entry form, first type in or import the client's name from a computerized database list. Make sure you're consistent about how you enter a client's name to avoid double counting and relying on multiple listings for this information. For example, don't list a client as "Gibson, Craig" one time and "Craig Gibson" another time.

- Refer to your "Industries Served" list to enter the industry in which this client serves and seeks his clients or customers.
- Enter the market data. Ideally, you would list the postal ZIP code in which the client is located and the city designation. There is much more market data available by ZIP than any other classification. You will use this information later in identifying target markets for special attention. Use a city or other designation if you already have geographical information assembled for the client.
- Refer to your "Services Provided" list and enter the names and dollars earned/to be earned for each service provided to this client during the current marketing period.
- Key in "Y" if this client makes referrals in your behalf.

FIGURE 3–1
Current Client Data Entry Form

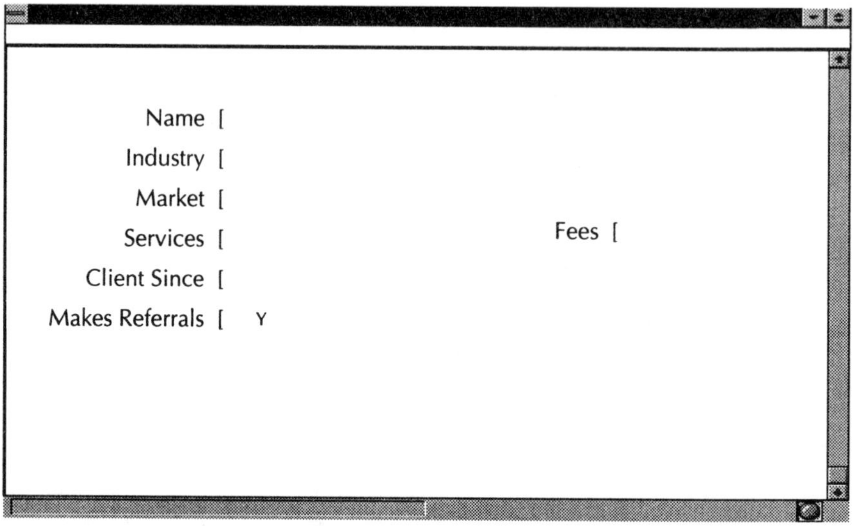

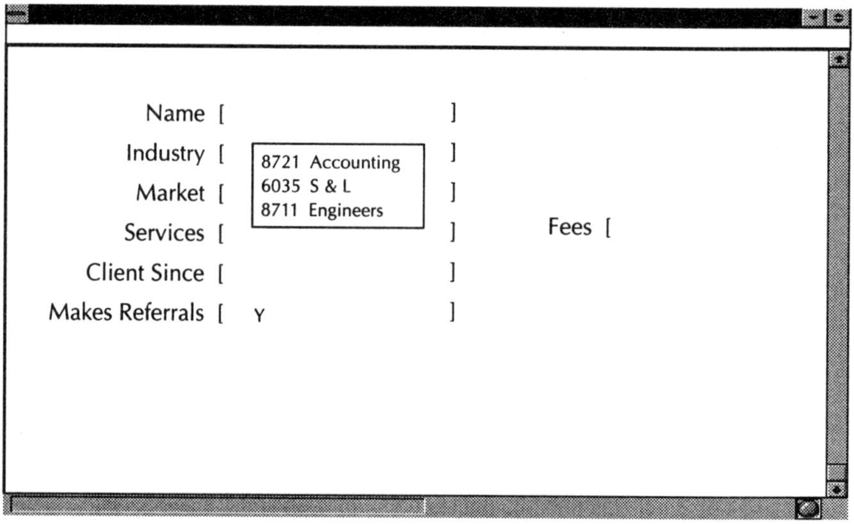

Current Prospect Data Entry

The next chart (Figure 3–2), called the Current Prospect Data Entry Form, again has three picklist fields. To complete the prospect data entry form, first type in or import the prospect's name.

FIGURE 3–2
Current Prospect Data Entry Form

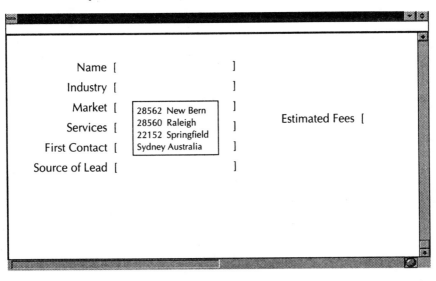

- Refer to your "Industries Served" list to enter the industry in which this prospect serves and seeks his prospects or customers.

- Enter the market data. Again, ideally, you would list the postal ZIP code in which the prospect is located. You will use this information later in identifying target markets for special attention.

- Refer to your "Services Provided" list and enter the names and dollars to be earned for each service provided to this prospect during the current marketing period.

- Enter the date of first contact so you can "age" your inventory of prospects you are seeking to convert into clients. Unlike a good wine, prospects seldom get better with time.

Current Leverage Relationship Data Entry

The Current Leverage Relationship Data Entry Form (Figure 3–3) introduces another field that lends itself to a picklist. The type of relationship can be client referral, nonclient referral, niche influential, or strategic alliance.

FIGURE 3–3
Current Leverage Relationship Data Entry Form

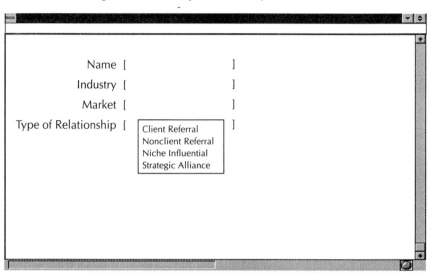

To complete Figure 3–3, the leverage relationship data entry form, as usual type in or import the contact's name.

- Refer to your "Industries Served" list to enter the Industry/SIC in which this leverage relationship provides you with leads.

- Enter the market/ZIP. List the postal ZIP code in which the leverage relationship is located. You will use this information later in identifying target markets for special attention.

- Determine the type of leverage relationship this person represents. You have four categories:

  Client referrals are those you currently serve who like and respect you and sing your praises to others.

  Nonclient referrals are represented by attorneys, bankers, and others in your market who are respected by your clients and prospects in your niche's industry and market and who give you leads, introduce you to prospects, and speak well of you to their colleagues.

  Niche influentials are key players in the niche's industry and market.

They include industry and market analysts, competitors, gurus, and editors of publications that are read by clients and prospects in the targeted niche. They are opinion leaders and trendsetters who serve, influence, and regulate members of the niche's industry and markets.

Strategic alliance partnerships are the relationships you have with individuals and organizations also serving the niche. Strategic alliance partners with whom you have a relationship offer complementary resources and marketing expertise.

PREPARING FOR DATA CRUNCHING

Visualizing the results you seek and what you will do with the results is essential. The beauty of our leveraged approach is that the few fields for which you entered data can be used in multiple reports. Figure 3–4 shows how the data that you enter now on your current clients, current prospects, and leverage relationships relates to the reports you'll be able to generate in subsequent chapters. Ultimately, your task will be to prepare a set of reports or profiles and a set of lists that you can use for different levels of analysis, planning, and control. Here is a roster of the reports you'll prepare in the following five chapters:

Figure 4–1   Current Clients Work Sheet

Figure 4–2   Personal Marketing Plan

Figure 5–1   Current Prospects Work Sheet

Figures 6–1   through 6–4
                Current Leverage Relationships Work Sheets

Figure 7–1   Services Provided Work Sheet

Figure 8–1   Personal Billing Performance

Figure 8–3   Current Served Industries Work Sheet

Figure 8–5   Current Served Markets Work Sheet

Naturally, each of these reports is discussed in the appropriate chapter. As you get to each chapter, we suggest that you make a copy

FIGURE 3–4
Relationship of Data Entry to Figures to Be Prepared

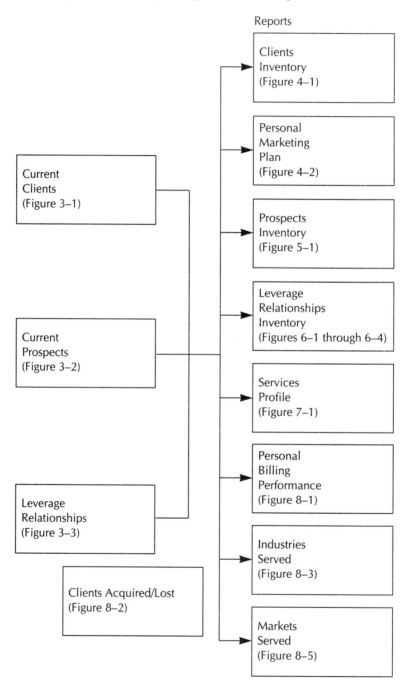

of each of the blank report forms to serve as a guide to what you need to prepare and to help you determine the computations to be performed.

This chapter has shown you the process for developing your client-centered database which will be used to analyze your current business for marketing advantage and leverage.

Each of the next five chapters will discuss the use of the featured report or reports.

CHAPTER 4

Evaluating Your Current Clients

This chapter shows you how to evaluate your current clients. The clients you serve are your revenue sources, and, as such, need to be managed to obtain maximum return from them.

On completion of this chapter, you will be able to:

☐ Determine the differences between an "A," "B," "C," "D," and "U" client.

☐ Determine clients who represent targets of attention and targets of opportunity.

☐ Understand why it's harmful to afford "C" and "D" clients the "A" level of service and attention.

☐ Begin developing your personal marketing plan.

PLANNING FOR THE EVALUATION TASK

To begin, please study Figure 4–1, Current Clients Work Sheet. Ideally, the data for Columns 1 through 5 is already logged in by the computer and hence you can print it at will. List each client's name in Column 1, the total revenue received from that client in Column 2a, and the percentage of total revenue that that client represents in Column 2b. It's best to list client revenue from the largest paying client to the smallest so you can readily analyze the makeup of your client base. Use Column 3 to list the client's four-digit SIC number, and Column 4 to list the client's ZIP. Place a "Y" in Column 5 if the client makes referrals on your behalf.

CRITERIA FOR CLASSIFYING YOUR CURRENT CLIENTS

To fill in Column 6 you need to know about classifying clients—a not-too-difficult assignment and sometimes a fun assignment.

Desirable Clients

1. "A" Clients: Clients that make referrals to others on your behalf, have strong potential for fee growth, are receptive to additional constructive service ideas, and frequently provide you with excellent opportunities to develop your skills and information base. Also include here "B" clients you hope will develop into "A" clients. They willingly pay their fees, are generally receptive to additional service discussions, and may be educated into making referrals at a later date.

2. "B" Clients: These clients are your bread-and-butter clients. They pay their bills and don't give you too much grief, but do not represent potential for good fee growth.

Unknown at This Time—"U" Clients

1. Clients whom you are now serving for the first time.

2. Newly acquired clients whom you are yet to begin serving.

3. Other existing clients not yet classified.

Undesirable Clients

1. "C" Clients: These clients seek discounts and additional free services and are frequently slow in paying invoices.

2. "D" Clients: These are the clients you wish you had never accepted in the first place. They often operate on the margin of ethical per-

FIGURE 4–1
Current Clients Work Sheet

1	2a	2b	3	4	5
Client	Revenue Dollars	Revenue %	SIC No.	ZIP Code	Referrals (Y or N)

Total: $_____   100%

formance and are not averse to pressuring you to compromise your personal and professional standards. You can't satisfy them, or they don't satisfy you!

Hence, in Column 6, classify each client as an "A," "B," "C," "D," or "U."

In Column 7, assess the current quality of the primary client-firm relationship with each client (shortened to quality of relationship or QoR). A score of 1 means you have a poor relationship. A score of 4 means the relationship is as sound as it can be. Any relationship that is assessed a 1 or 2 automatically becomes a target of attention (Column 9); place the letter "A" there. Also, immediately enter this client's name under the targets of attention heading on your personal marketing plan (Figure 4–2).

In Column 8, you estimate the likelihood of providing additional services during the current marketing period. Put an "L" in the column if it is likely that you will provide additional services. This client becomes a target of opportunity and should be listed on the personal marketing plan.

Column 9 requires that you identify targets of attention and targets

6	7	8	9	10
Client Class	Quality of Relationship	Additional Services	Target Categories	Comments, Next Steps

of opportunity. Hence, in Column 9, you assign the appropriate target classification for the remaining clients.

A target of opportunity consists of existing "A" and "B" clients with needs, the budget to pay for need satisfaction, and the willingness to invest the funds.

Remember, not every client will receive a target classification. The goal of targeting is to enable you to leverage your time by identifying which clients require special attention and handling at this time.

In Column 10, list other steps you need to take, given your assessments.

Your Personal Marketing Plan

We also suggest that you create a personal marketing plan or PMP file (see Figure 4–2) on your word processing program or askSam if you are using that program. This is so you'll simply have more room on which to list your intended actions and to track your performance and results.

With this minimum bit of preparation completed you are now ready to begin classifying your clients as a basis for taking the appropriate action with each.

FIGURE 4–2
Sample Personal Marketing Plan Form

PERSONAL MARKETING PLAN

From __/__ to __/__

1. Targets of Opportunity:

2. Targets of Attention:

3. Targets of Influence:

4. Promotion:

5. Prospecting:

6. Other Marketing Actions:

ANALYZING YOUR COMPLETED
"CURRENT CLIENTS WORK SHEET"

You now have a valuable document that can provide you with a wealth of information about the nature and scope of your current base of clients. We've developed a set of questions you need to ask and answer for yourself.

1. How many clients are you serving? Choose from these options:
   - I'm overloaded!
   - I'm as busy as I want to be.
   - I'm busy, but I could serve more without strain.
   - I'm not busy, and I need to do more.
2. How many clients does it take to generate 70 to 80 percent of total revenue? What percent of clients is this?
3. What is the nature of your client base?
   - You have a cluster client base if 20 to 30 percent of your clients account for 70 to 80 percent of total revenue.
   - Otherwise you have a volume client base.

   Note: See Chapter 8 for the strategic implications of a cluster or volume client base.
4. How many clients in each class do you have?
   - Is there a balance?
   - Do you have too many "C" or "D" clients?
5. How many of your "C" and "D" clients receive "A" or "B" level of attention, and why do you allow this to happen? Are you worried about losing them, or that they may bad-mouth you to their friends?

WORKING WITH THE RESULTS OF YOUR ANALYSIS

We have developed the following strategies for leveraging your current clients. Please don't skip this section or disregard those strategies that you happen not to like at first reading. Each has proved effective during our work with thousands of professionals just like you.

Leverage and Protect the "A"s

Your "A" clients need to account for a substantial portion of your revenue and provide you with new revenue opportunities. Remember, an "A" is an extremely desirable client. This type of client is often sought by competitors, tends to be knowledgeable about buying and using services, and requires "A+" level of attention.

Upgrade the "B"s

Review Column 6 and identify "B" clients who may have potential for additional services if you invest some time in educating them about the need for your services. Note any actions to take in Column 7, and list the client's name under the targets of opportunity heading on your personal marketing plan.

Work with the "C"s

Your "C" clients make their presence known quickly as they haggle over fees, want scope-of-work changes without paying you for the extra time, and give you the "check is in the mail" routine when you bring past notices to their attention. These clients can be grouped in two categories:

"C"clients with potential for upgrading. These become targets of attention. Examine your feelings and justifications for the way you handle the money side of the relationship. For example, if you gave in during the initial fee negotiations, you inadvertently educated the client that "Fees are not important enough to me to stand my ground." Or, "You are the boss when it comes to financial discussions."

If you are tense or uncertain, you may cave in when the client wants to change the scope of the engagement without renegotiating the financial terms, or you may be unwilling to call the client to clear an unpaid balance. Check out your rationale. Is it, "I need this client's revenue so I had better not get the client upset with me"?

To turn matters around, accept responsibility for the situation and systematically reeducate the client by pointing out that conditions have changed and that the relationship needs to be reconstructed. Verify this understanding in writing and don't depart from your new understanding. List the actions you will take to reeducate this client about the value received from your solutions and assistance on the PMP.

"C" clients with no potential for upgrading. It's decision time. Can you afford to keep this client? Is it worth the hassle and upset? If you decide it's time to cut the cord, do so gently and firmly, stressing the need for payment in full or more fees for the services you are rendering. If you choose not to sever the relationship, at least prepare and send a letter that spells out the terms of your relationship, scope of your services, and responsibilities to one another. When there are outstanding balances, we require up-

front monies from some of our clients in order to conduct new assignments.

Drop the "D"s

Too often, troublesome clients receive "A"-level attention, and, as a result, you have educated them that their attitude and behaviors pay off. Perhaps more significantly, you literally steal time and attention from your best clients. When dealing with "D" clients your actions steps are clear:

1. Determine the sources of such troublesome clients and correct them immediately. If you are getting such clients from referrals, educate the referring parties as to the preferred type of client sought.

2. Identify the relatively few problem clients that you *must* retain because of the impact dropping them could have on relationships with key clients and others. Be realistic—these situations are few and far between.

3. Identify candidates for termination. For every "D" hour terminated, you'll gain hours more energy and enjoyment. One client told us, "Five minutes with Mr. X is equal to two hours in purgatory." If you feel uncomfortable, ask yourself, "If not already a client, would I accept this party as a new client?" If the answer is no, Hasta la vista Baby!

4. Analyze the cause(s) of your "D" client situations. Are you getting these clients from a particular referral source? Are you uncomfortable in handling the give-and-take of affairs with them?

Pay Attention to the "U"s

Your goal is to classify every client as soon as you can so you can take the appropriate next steps. Make every client currently designated as "U" a target of attention and list their names on your personal marketing plan.

ASSESSMENT PAYS OFF

If you're like most professionals, you have probably never assessed and listed your clients in the manner described in this chapter.

Yet, after doing so, you'll readily see that assessment of the present client base is essential for understanding the nature of your practice and for beginning to develop a framework for attracting more "A" and "B" clients.

Now please turn to Chapter 5, which discusses procedures for evaluating prospects that you are tracking.

CHAPTER 5

Evaluating Your Prospects in Hand

Prospects, as we've discussed already, represent nonclient organizations, associations, and individuals with whom you have had a serious discussion about a hot-button need and your proposed solution. Because of their importance and potential for adding to your firm's revenues, prospects are automatically classified as targets of opportunity.

After completing the actions recommended in this chapter, you will be able to:

☐ Assess the worth of your existing prospects.

☐ Devise a plan for converting them into new clients.

PLANNING FOR THE EVALUATION TASK

Please examine Figure 5–1. It is a convenient form to use in evaluating your prospects. To use this form effectively, list the prospect's name in Column 1, the date of first contact in Column 2, the industry in which the prospect operates in Column 3, the market in which this prospect resides in Column 4, the service offered in Column 5, and estimated revenue in Column 6.

In Column 7, estimate the potential for conversion on a scale from

FIGURE 5–1
Current Prospects Work Sheet

CURRENT PROSPECTS

1	2	3	4
Prospect	Date of First Contact	Industry	Market

0 (none) to 100 percent (pure certainty). Finally, in Column 8, give your plan for converting this prospect. Make a copy of your personal marketing plan, or simply use the copy you worked with in evaluating your current clients in Chapter 4. List your specific actions in your PMP. Be certain to list the "what," "who," and "when."

YOUR FUTURE IS IN YOUR PROSPECT LIST

Your current prospect list, when completed, is a powerful marketing profile. You'll be glad you prepared such an inventory for your practice because it shows at a glance what the health of your business is in terms of potential new clients. To get even more value from your analysis, consider these questions:

1. How many prospects do I have?

2. What estimated dollar value do they represent, each and in total?

3. Do the estimated dollars meet my revenue goals?

_/_ to _/_

5	6	7	8
Service Offered	Estimated Revenue	Potential for Conversion (0 to 100%)	Plan for Converting

4. Will the estimated revenue offset fees known or suspected to be lost from clients during this period?
5. What SICs are the prospects in? Are they my target industries?
6. What sources generate the prospects—referrals, self-initiated, my reputation, other?
7. What level of attention is required to get or convert each?
8. What priorities for follow-up are there?

To a large extent, the number and quality of your current prospects determine what tomorrow's practice will become. Your goal, at all times, is to keep your potential new business pipeline full and flowing with high-potential "clones" of your best clients. The subject of prospecting will be covered fully in Chapter 27.

MOVE INTO ACTION

Because each prospect is automatically classified as a target of opportunity, your task is to list each name on the PMP. So once again review the questions listed above and add to your PMP any new actions that come to mind that you need to take.

You have now completed an essential evaluation step in ultimately marketing your consulting or professional services effectively. You never want to take your prospect situation for granted. Each prospect is a wasting asset if you fail to capitalize on the potential within each prospective client situation.

In Chapter 6, we'll guide you in managing your current leverage relationships to help you generate and identify even more prospects, and do a fine job of serving your clients.

CHAPTER 6

Managing Your Current Leverage Relationships

Leverage relationships refer to individuals with whom you have a relationship that results in a disproportionate (highly favorable) return to you for marketing purposes. Leverage relationships help you in terms of introductions, leads, and vouch-for-you statements to prospects and others with whom you need or want to make a favorable impression. This is a relatively lengthy chapter, but we urge you not to shortcut the recommended actions. Leverage relationships are valuable relationships that enable you to leverage your time and resources.

Upon completion of this chapter you will be able to answer the following questions:

☐ What are the four classes of leverage relationships?
☐ What are the benefits of building leverage relationships?
☐ What is the best way to manage these important relationships?

PAYOFFS FROM BUILDING LEVERAGE RELATIONSHIPS

As you saw in Chapter 2, there are four classes of leverage relationships: client referrals, nonclient referrals, niche influentials, and strategic alliances.

Building and maintaining an active leverage relationship program produces several key benefits and makes your new business development task easier for three solid reasons:

1. Satisfied clients have firsthand knowledge of the services your firm provides, and can communicate this knowledge to other professionals in an objective manner that is not tainted by self-interest. No hard sell is required. A client referral allows you to work well within the range of your comfort zone. A satisfied client active in the business community is a low-cost form of advertising that enhances your self-esteem.

2. Nonclient referrals and niche influentials enable you to become known to suspects and prospects through introductions and referrals. Because niche influentials are at the "pulse" of the industry, relationships with them can pay you great dividends in obtaining insider information.

3. Strategic alliances enable you to build virtual organizations comprised of specialized resources you need without having to invest heavily in in-house resources.

MANAGING YOUR CURRENT CLIENT REFERRAL SOURCES

By following the practical approach laid out here, you will ensure the development and maintenance of a valuable asset—your current client referral sources.

Inventory Your Client Referrals

Figure 6–1 is a convenient form you can use as an inventory of current clients who make referrals in your behalf. This form is easily prepared by the computer processing the data you entered in Figure 3–1, Current Client Data Entry Form. List the client's name in Column 1, the industry in Column 2, and the market in Column 3.

Analyze the Inventory and Take Action

To complete the analysis of your client referral sources, in Column 4 consider the type of referral source they represent. Do they initiate leads and referrals, or are they the more passive vouch-for types? If a client does not initiate in your behalf, place an "X" in the No column. Immediately list this client's name in the target of attention section of your personal marketing plan. Your goal is to determine why such clients don't initiate and to take appropriate steps for educating them to do so.

Still in Column 4, if this client is an initiator, indicate the level of effort the client invests in your behalf in the Yes column. An "A" in the Yes column means that this client is a continuing/recurring referral source initiating in your behalf. In effect, this client is an unpaid sales person for you and needs to be afforded the proper level of attention.

A "B" identifies a sporadic source.

A "C" identifies a one-time-only referral source. List this client's name in the target of attention section of your PMP. Your goal is to determine why this client no longer gives you referrals.

In Column 5, assess the current quality of relationship with each client referral source. Using a scale of from 1 (for a poor relationship) up to 4 (for a perfect relationship), assign the proper number to each and place this number in Column 5. Any relationship assessed a 1 or 2 automatically becomes a target of attention.

In Column 6, estimate the potential for providing referrals both short-term (in the current marketing period) and long-term (beyond the current marketing period). Use an "H" for high potential, "M" for medium potential, and "L" for low potential. Put the appropriate letters in the short-term an long-term columns of Column 6.

In Column 7, determine the appropriate target classification for each client. Use "TO" for target of opportunity and "TA" for target of attention. You may have to use both target designations. List the referral's name on your PMP, and spell out in detail how you plan to use this valuable relationship.

Assess Your Client Referrals Base

Once your inventory analysis is complete, consider the following questions:

- How many of my clients make referrals?
- How many initiators do I have?

FIGURE 6–1
Current Client Referral Sources Work Sheet

1	2	3	4	
			Initiate?	
Client Name	Industry/SIC	Market/ZIP	Yes*	No

*Level of Effort
  A=continuing
  B=sporadic
  C=one time only

- How frequently do I acknowledge clients who make referrals for me?
- Which referrals might be drying up, and why?
- Which clients who don't now make referrals should?

Determine the required actions derived from pondering these questions and, as before, list them on your PMP.

MANAGING YOUR CURRENT NONCLIENT REFERRAL SOURCES

Nonclients who make referrals in your behalf include accountants serving the niche, alums of your firm, attorneys, bankers, investment brokers, and real estate agents.

Inventory Your Nonclient Referrals

Use Figure 6–2 to make an inventory of current nonclients who make referrals in your behalf. This form is easily prepared by the com-

5	6		7
Quality of Relationship 1–4**	Potential†		Target Classification Opportunity/Attention
	Short-Term	Long-Term	

**Quality of Relationship
  1=poor
  4=perfect

†Potential
  H=high
  M=medium
  L=low

puter processing the data you entered in Figure 3–3, Current Leverage Relationship Data Entry Form. List the referral's name in Column 1, the industry in Column 2, and the market in Column 3.

Analyze the Inventory and Take Action

To complete the analysis of your current nonclient referral sources, classify the type of source they represent. Do they initiate leads and referrals, or are they the more passive vouch-for types? If this referral source does not initiate in your behalf, place an "X" in the No column of Column 4. List this person's name in the target of attention section of your PMP. Your goal is to determine why some referral sources don't initiate, and to take appropriate steps for educating them to do so.

If you designate this referral source as "Yes" for being an initiator, list the level of effort invested in your behalf in the Yes column. Once again, an "A" in the Yes column means that this person is a continuing/recurring referral source initiating in your behalf. In effect this client is an unpaid sales person for you and needs to be afforded the proper level of attention.

FIGURE 6–2
Current Nonclient Referral Sources Work Sheet

1	2	3	4	
			Initiate?	
Name	Industry/SIC	Market/ZIP	Yes*	No

*Level of Effort
  A=continuing
  B=sporadic
  C=one time only

A "B" identifies a sporadic source.

A "C" identifies a one-time only referral source. List this person's name in the target of attention section of your PMP. Your goal is to determine why this source no longer gives you referrals.

Complete the remaining columns using the rationale you applied in Figure 6–1.

Once your inventory analysis is complete, you will want to consider the following questions:

- How many nonclient referral sources do I have?
- How many initiators do I have?
- How frequently do I acknowledge nonclients who make referrals for me?
- Which referrals might be drying up, and why?

Then list on your PMP the required actions that become evident.

5	6		7
Quality of Relationship 1–4**	Potential†		Target Classification Opportunity/Attention
	Short-Term	Long-Term	

**Quality of Relationship
  1=poor
  4=perfect

†Potential
  H=high
  M=medium
  L=low

MANAGING YOUR CURRENT RELATIONSHIPS WITH NICHE INFLUENTIALS

Niche influentials can play an important role in your marketing activities. NIs include industry and market analysts, competitors, gurus, and editors of publications that are read by clients and prospects.

Inventory Your Niche Influentials

Use Figure 6–3 to build an inventory of niche influentials with whom you have a relationship.

Analyze and Assess

To complete the analysis of your current niche influentials, proceed as you have for Figures 6–1 and 6–2. Complete Figure 6–3 by spelling out in detail how you plan to use these valuable relationships. This information will be used to build your PMP.

FIGURE 6–3
Niche Influentials Work Sheet

1	2	3	4	
			Initiate?	
Name	Industry/SIC	Market/ZIP	Yes*	No

*Level of Effort
  A=continuing
  B=sporadic
  C=one time only

Once your inventory analysis is complete, consider these now-familiar questions:

- How many niche influentials do I have?
- How many initiators do I have?
- How frequently do I acknowledge niche influentials who make referrals for me?
- Which referrals might be drying up, and why?

Then list on your PMP the appropriate actions derived from pondering these questions.

MANAGING YOUR CURRENT RELATIONSHIPS WITH STRATEGIC ALLIANCE PARTNERS

Strategic alliance partners are cooperative relationships you have with individuals and organizations serving your niche with whom you of-

5	6		7
Quality of Relationship 1–4**	Potential†		Plan for Leveraging This Relationship
	Short-Term	Long-Term	

**Quality of Relationship
 1=poor
 4=perfect

†Potential
 H=high
 M=medium
 L=low

fer complementary services. Pooling resources and experience with others who serve the niche can help you create market offerings that are in demand by clients and high-potential prospects.

Inventory Your Strategic Alliance Partners

Use Figure 6–4 to build an inventory of strategic alliance partners with whom you have a relationship.

Analyze and Assess

To complete the analysis of your current strategic alliance partners, you know the routine. Assess the current quality of relationship with each strategic alliance partner in Column 4. Using a scale of from 1 (for a poor relationship) up to 4 (for a perfect relationship), assign the proper number to each and place this number in Column 4. Any relationship assessed a 1 or 2 automatically becomes a target of attention. Spell out how you plan to leverage each relationship and list your actions on the PMP.

FIGURE 6–4
Strategic Alliance Partners Work Sheet

1	2	3	4	5
Name and Affiliation	Industry/SIC	Market/ZIP	Quality of Relationship 1–4*	Plan for Leveraging This Relationship

*Quality of Relationship
1=poor
4=perfect

Then review the key questions and list on your PMP the required actions derived from pondering the questions:

- How many strategic alliance partners do I have in each industry?
- How often do I acknowledge strategic alliance partners who make referrals for me?
- Which alliance relationships might be drying up, and why?

Now that you have completed your analysis and action planning with all four categories of your leverage relationships, it's time to move on to Chapter 7, where we'll focus on your services offering.

CHAPTER 7

Sizing Up Your Services

The services you offer and provide to your clients and prospective clients must be perceived as adding value to the operations of the buyer. In this chapter we'll examine your services from two important viewpoints—yours and your client's.

After completing the exercises in this chapter you will be able to:

☐ Prepare a profile of your current services to determine the attractiveness of each service to your desirable clients.

☐ Determine which services are to be designated as targets of attention.

☐ Prepare a client-centered service analysis that you will use in personal selling contacts and in preparing promotional materials.

PREPARING YOUR CURRENT SERVICES PROFILE

Figure 7–1 provides you with a practical form for assessing the nature and scope of your current services. Using this form requires that you:

1. Rank your services from the largest revenues to the smallest revenues during the most recent 12 months, and list each service by name in Column 1.

2. List all the fees obtained from each service in Column 2.

FIGURE 7–1
Current Services Profile

	1	2	3
	Services	Fees from Services	% of Total Fees
1.		$	%
2.		$	%
3.		$	%
4.		$	%
5.		$	%
6.		$	%
7.		$	%
8.		$	%
9.		$	%
10.		$	%
11.		$	%
12.		$	%
	Total Fees	$	100%

*Class I = Value-adding solution
Class II = Recurring service

3. Compute the total fees and determine the percentage of total fees from each service. Enter this percentage in Column 3.

4. Determine whether each service can be classified as *leading edge, competitive,* or *falling behind* in terms of technology, client acceptance, and your interest in providing the service. Place an "X" in the appropriate column under the analysis designation in Column 4a, 4b, or 4c.

5. Determine whether each service is seen as a Class I or Class II service by your clients and prospective clients, and place an "X" in the appropriate column under the class designation in Column 5a or 5b.

6. Jot your comments and implications ideas in Column 6.

You've now completed an important analysis of your services. In general, you want to be able to position your services as Class I, leading

4 Analysis			5 Class*		6
a. Leading Edge	b. Competitive	c. Falling Behind	a. I	b. II	Comments/ Implications

edge solutions to important needs and problems. Services that you deem necessary for continued survival of your practice, but are perceived by clients as falling behind in terms of technology and attractiveness, need to be classified as targets of attention, and the appropriate level of attention and resources allocated to them.

DEVELOPING A CLIENT-CENTERED VIEW OF YOUR SERVICES

Now let's develop a client-centered view of the services you provide. The insights gained as a result of this analysis will serve you well in selling additional services to your clients and prospective clients. The understanding will also be useful in preparing written promotional and proposal-related documents.

A professional service is largely an intangible idea that is purchased for the end results it will produce. As stated previously, clients don't really purchase services; they purchase the expectations of receiving a more favorable future. The future contains expected benefits to the purchaser.

Benefits exist solely in the perception of the client. Benefits are always related to the client's needs and expectations about the way in which those needs and expectations will be met.

Figure 7–2, Client-Centered Service Analysis, can be used to identify benefits that are important to clients and, indeed, to force you to view services as your clients and prospective clients perceive them.

To use the form effectively, follow these steps:

1. Enter the name of the service you want to analyze on the top line.

2. Move to the upper left-hand block, "Improve or Enhance," and ask: "In what ways does this service enable purchasers or users to improve or enhance something they value?" List your answers in the block—for example, "improve market penetration," "enhance image," and so on.

3. Move next to the upper right-hand block and ask: "In what ways does this service reduce, relieve, or eliminate some unwanted condition?" List your answers in the block—for example, "reduce filing time," "relieve backlog pressures," and so forth.

4. Move to the "Protect" block and ask: "In what ways does this service enable the purchaser or users to protect something they value?" Again, list your answers in the block.

5. Then move to the remaining blocks and complete them in a similar manner.

Note: Not all blocks need to be or will be completed for a given service.

You now have a set of potential benefits that can accrue to a client. The completed chart can be used in proposal writing and face-to-face discussions with clients and training staff.

Other key service words and phrases that could be used in filling out the client-centered service analysis are as follows:

FIGURE 7–2
Client-Centered Service Analysis

For: _____
(Service)

Your task is to identify client needs and problem situations for which your service is appropriate. For each verb listed below, identify how your service applies. For example, under the word "eliminate" you might put "unnecessary forms and procedures."

Improve or Enhance	Reduce, Relieve, or Eliminate
Protect	Restructure
Identify, Develop, or Install	Restore or Resolve

Improve

Decision-making capability.	Understanding of costs.
Profits.	Appearance.
Cash flow position.	Information for decisions.
Through-put time.	Credit rating.

Internal operations.
Public product image.
Quality, reliability, effectiveness
of software.
Usefulness and relevance of
documentation.
Operating efficiency and
productivity.

User service needs.
Long-term outlook.
Competitive capabilities.
Employee morale and motivation.
Employee safety.
Market position.
Use of computer equipment.

Enhance

Credibility of client's role in
community.
User orientation of software.
Service to particular groups or
users.
Inherent advantages.
Shareholder value.
Competitive edge.
Utilization of equipment and
facilities.

Employee morale and motivation.
Working capital position.
Organizational image.
Technical understanding of
problem.
Existing strengths and image.
Status in peer group.
Existing skills.
Multinational marketing
opportunities.

Reduce

Number of internal and external
conflicts.
Costs.
Deficits.
Downtime.
Skills levels requirements.
Service delays and unreliability.

Excess capacity.
Idle equipment time.
Peaking of demands.
Risk.
Waste.
Inefficiency.
Tax liabilities.

Relieve

Conflict.
Congestion.
Public pressure and adverse
opinions.
Recurring problems.

Future cost pressures.
Pressure and tension.
Organization conflicts.
Blockages to staff development.
Undue workload.

Eliminate

Errors.
Bottlenecks.
Misappropriation of resources.
Constraints.
Headaches.
Adverse criticisms.
Low cost-benefit ratios.

Extra paperwork.
Cumbersome routines.
Pilferage and internal security
  problems.
Shortsightedness.
Unnecessary costs.

Protect

Client reputation and integrity.
Independence.
Assets.
Market position and market share.

Security of product served.
Proprietary information.
Integrity and public image.
Self-interests.

Restructure

Organization.
Current operations.
Work flow.
Planning process.
Reporting systems.

Compensation and incentive
  program.
Operating mechanisms.
Internal operations.

Identify, Develop, or Install

Strategies.
Key problem areas.
Decision factors.
Unforeseen opportunities.
Solutions to problem areas.
Needs.

Available resources.
Alternatives or options.
Constraints or limits.
Market shifts.
Potentials.

Restore or Resolve

Profitable operations.
Role of organization in
  community.
Standardized development process.
Deteriorating facilities and
  equipment.
Long-term outlook.

Markets, competitive edge, and
  profits.
Management structure.
Employee morale/motivation.
Market penetration.
Outdated skills.

FIGURE 7–3
Completed Client-Centered Service Analysis

For _____ *Audit Services* _____
(Service)

Your task is to identify client needs and problem situations for which your service is appropriate. For each verb listed below, identify how your service applies. For example, under the word "eliminate" you might put "unnecessary forms and procedures."

Improve or Enhance	*Reduce, Relieve, or Eliminate*
Cash flow	Exposure to loss
Profitability	Paperwork
Accounting procedures	Bottlenecks
Operations	Investment debt
Revenues	Material errors
Internal control	Errors
Internal reporting	
Protect	*Restructure*
Assets	Quality of reporting system
Credibility	Unprofitable operations
Reputation	Unnecessary reports
Profit	Branch operations
Lines of credit	
Liquidity	
Identify, Develop, Install	*Restore or Resolve*
External reporting	Image of client
Management information	Reliability of financial
system	statements
Cost systems	Resolve backlogs, uncertainty,
Decision-making model	inefficiencies, management
	anxiety

A sample of how an accountant might complete Figure 7–2 for an audit service is presented in Figure 7–3.

With this important chapter behind us, let's move now into an examination of your strategic profile.

CHAPTER 8

Building Your Firm's Strategic Profile

Clients come and go, and the strategic position of your business changes accordingly. In today's volatile environment it's essential to know and capitalize on the strategic implications of your current client, industry, and market mix. This chapter presents an approach for building your firm's strategic profile.

Determining your current strategic position involves a wide-angle, "macro-level" analysis of your current business as a whole using simple analytical techniques. Later chapters will focus on micro issues such as client groups and individual players, such as targets of opportunity and the like.

Upon completion of this chapter you will be able to:

☐ Build a strategic profile for your current and probable future business.

☐ Determine the strategic implications of the direction in which your business is heading.

☐ Determine the strategic implications of your current client mix.

☐ Make strategic decisions about changing the direction and/or client mix.

STRATEGIC PROFILE COMPONENTS

Every business has its own, unique strategic position, which is comprised of three components:

1. *Momentum:* Your business is either stable or it is growing or declining at some rate of change.
2. *Direction:* Your practice is headed somewhere as a result of the industries (SICs) and market ZIPs in which you serve and seek clients.
3. *Client mix:* The number and types of clients drives the strategic profile.

THE BIG "MO"— DETERMINING THE MOMENTUM OF YOUR BUSINESS/PRACTICE

The momentum of your firm is fueled by the revenue generated from your clients—your billing performance—and is impacted by the amount of client churn—the number of clients you gain and lose during a period. Let's look at your billing performance first.

Your Personal Billing Performance

Figure 8–1, Personal Billing Performance, is used to record your revenue history. Enter the billing performance for the most recent three- to five-year period (or if you've been in business for less than 36 months, for as long as you've been in practice).

Let's take a strategic look at your results by considering these questions:

1. Is your business stable? If yes,

   - Are you surprised? Is this by choice or chance?
   - What is the probability of slipping into decline—high, medium, or low? On what do you base this assessment?
   - What plans do you have for either breaking out of a stable condition and into a growth mode, or preventing sliding into a declining mode? List these actions now in your PMP so you don't overlook them.

FIGURE 8–1
Personal Billing Performance

Year	No. of Billed Hours	Revenue ($)	Growth (%)

2. Are you enjoying a growth situation? If yes,

- Are you working harder, but you could work smarter (such as leveraging your time, talents, and technology)?

- Can you recruit, train, coach, and retain the staff you need?

- Are you building a "virtual organization" capability by forming strategic alliances with others who serve your targeted niches? If not, why not? What justification do you have for not availing yourself of this talent?

- Are you managing more, billing fewer hours, but at higher rates? If not, what plans do you have for realizing this goal? List them now on your PMP inventory.

3. Is your business in a declining mode? If yes,

- Are you surprised?

- Is the decline within your tolerance limits?

- Are you aware of the reasons for the decline? What plans do you have for breaking out of this mode? List them on your PMP now.

Your Client Churn Picture

Clients come and go for a variety of reasons. It's in your best interest to track your client churn so you can capitalize on opportunities and head off threats. Use Figure 8–2, Clients Acquired/Lost Profile, to tabulate:

FIGURE 8–2
Clients Acquired/ Lost Profile

Date: From:_____ to:_____

Clients Acquired			Clients Lost		
Source	Number	Fee	Reasons	Number	Fee
Client referrals	____	____	Work completed	____	____
Leads from			Fee complaint	____	____
recommendations	____	____	Service complaint	____	____
Walk-ins/image	____	____	Moved from area	____	____
Targeted action	____	____	Merged or acquired	____	____
Advertising	____	____	Business sold	____	____
Unknown	____	____	Bankruptcy	____	____
			Outside pressure		
			Bank	____	____
			Government	____	____
			Other	____	____
			Unknown	____	____
Totals	____	____	Totals	____	____

1. The number of clients you acquired during a given marketing period.
2. The sources of clients you acquired.
3. The dollar value of clients you acquired.
4. The number of clients you lost during a given marketing period.
5. The reason for the losses.
6. The dollar value of clients you lost.

Figure 8–2 is vital because it shows both the sources of new clients that have been most effective for you, and the severity of the factors that led to your losing clients. This analysis reveals a picture of the health of your practice. With this information at hand you have a clear picture of the marketing and client retention job ahead of you. List actions to take on your PMP inventory.

We turn next to determining the direction of your business, an essential leveraging step that results in sharpening your prospecting activities.

DETERMINING THE DIRECTION OF YOUR BUSINESS

The current direction of your business is driven by the industries (SICs) and market ZIPs in which you serve and seek clients.

Profiling Your Current Industry Mix

Use Figure 8–3 to profile the industries in which you both seek and serve clients. You can then refer to the completed from to analyze your industry mix by considering:

1. The number of industries served:

   - How many industries do you now serve? (Column 1)

   - How many industries make up 70 to 80 percent of total revenue? (Column 4)

2. The nature of the industry mix:

   - Do you have a volume or cluster industry mix? (See Figure 8–4.)

     A volume industry mix is characterized by a relatively large number of industries, each of which constitutes a relatively small percentage of total fees.

     A cluster industry mix is characterized by a relatively small number of industries, each of which constitutes a relatively large percentage of total fees.

   - Do you have a diverse or related industry mix? (See Figure 8–4.)

     A diverse industry mix is comprised of a large number of different types of industries.

     A related industry mix is comprised of industries that are more similar than different in structure and purpose.

FIGURE 8–3
Analyzing Your Industry Mix

1	2	3	4	5
Industry	No. of Clients	Revenue Earned	% of Total Revenue	No. of Prospects

3. The current penetration:

   - How many clients do you have in each industry?
   - How many prospects do you have in each industry?

4. What are the strategic implications of your industry mix?

Figure 8–4 shows the advantages and disadvantages of volume or cluster and related or diverse industry mixes. List any actions suggested by this figure on your PMP.

Profiling Your Current Market Mix

Use Figure 8–5 to profile the market ZIPs in which you serve and seek clients. You can use your PC to easily prepare this for your analysis.

Let's analyze your market base by considering:

1. How many different market ZIPs do you serve? Which ZIPs have the most clients and prospects in them? Do you have a dense or sparse market mix?

   A dense market has a large number of clients and a large base of prospects for you to contact.

   A sparse market has a relatively small number of clients and prospects in it.

6	7	8
Estimated New Revenue	Growth Potential	Notes

2. What are the strategic implications of your market mix? List any actions suggested by your analysis on your PMP inventory.

DETERMINING THE NATURE OF YOUR CLIENT BASE

Your clients probably come in many sizes, you may have lots or few of them, they may be in related industries, and you may have too many undesirable clients acquired during earlier times. Your client mix represents the current and future revenue sources and needs to be studied thoroughly to leverage the results available from them. To best determine the nature of your client base, we need to return to Figure 4–1, Current Clients Work Sheet, presented in Chapter 4. With the chart handy, answer the following as it becomes apparent:

1. What is the nature of your client base? (The nature of your client base can be characterized as a volume client base or a cluster client base.)

   - You have a cluster client base if 20 to 30 percent of your clients account for 70 to 80 percent of total revenue.

   - Otherwise you have a volume client base.

2. What are the strategic implications of your client mix? Figure 8–4

FIGURE 8–4
Implications of Your Existing Clients and Industry Mix

VOLUME OR CLUSTER CLIENT BASE

VOLUME

Advantages

- Loss of any one client is not severe; volume spreads risk.
- Workload is spread out and avoids peaks and valleys.
- More exposure to more industries results.
- More visibility is gained.
- Acceptance of poor client is less risky.
- Staff is exposed to varied client situations.

Disadvantages

- Volume is harder to manage.
- More deadlines must be met.
- You have less contact with each client.
- More collection problems are likely.
- You have less chance for business development.
- Being all things to all people is impossible.
- More staff is required.
- With less opportunity for specialization, you may be seen as offering "me-too" service.

CLUSTER

Advantages

- Specialization can enable better service.
- A cluster mix is easier to manage.
- Staff training may be better.
- You have more contact with each client.
- Specialized skills can be promoted to targeted people.

Disadvantages

- Greater staff training is required.
- It is more expensive to replace staff.
- Deadlines may be concentrated at certain dates.
- You may encounter partner difficulties in managing larger engagements.
- Partner jurisdiction/fiefdom problems may arise.

DIVERSE OR RELATED CLIENT BASE

DIVERSE

Advantages

- Diversity spreads risk.
- Growth rate may be faster initially.
- Current direction may continue.

Disadvantages

- Engagement often becomes a routine "me-too" engagement.
- Partners are often spread too thin to develop perspective.

FIGURE 8–4 Continued

- Value of management is diminished.
- Broad is not necessarily better.

RELATED
Advantages
- Specialization is possible.
- More client-centered information is available.
- Information is easier to acquire and manage.

Disadvantages
- You may encounter competition from larger, more aggressive firms.
- You may be vulnerable to industry and markets drying up.

FIGURE 8–5
Current Market/ZIP Mix

Market/ZIP	Revenue		Penetration	
	$	% of Total	No. of Clients	No. of Prospects

shows the advantages and disadvantages of a cluster and volume client mix. List any actions suggested by this figure on your PMP Inventory.

You have now completed an analysis of your business/practice that will yield many benefits as you identify the actions suggested by the analysis.

We turn now to Part Three, which deals with your targets of opportunity, targets of attention, and targets of influence.

PART THREE
Targets

CHAPTER 9

Managing Your Targets of Opportunity

This chapter brings together the results of your previous inventory and analysis actions. Now you are ready to learn more about working effectively with your targets of opportunity.

In this chapter you'll learn how to determine:

☐ What targets of opportunity are there in my practice?

☐ How do I best capitalize on the potential they represent?

☐ What should by my continuing goals?

YOUR PRESENT OPPORTUNITIES

Figure 9–1 presents the full range of opportunities available within your business. You'll want to review this figure periodically to ensure that you are not overlooking any opportunities that might not be readily apparent.

FIGURE 9–1
Targets of Opportunity and Related Actions

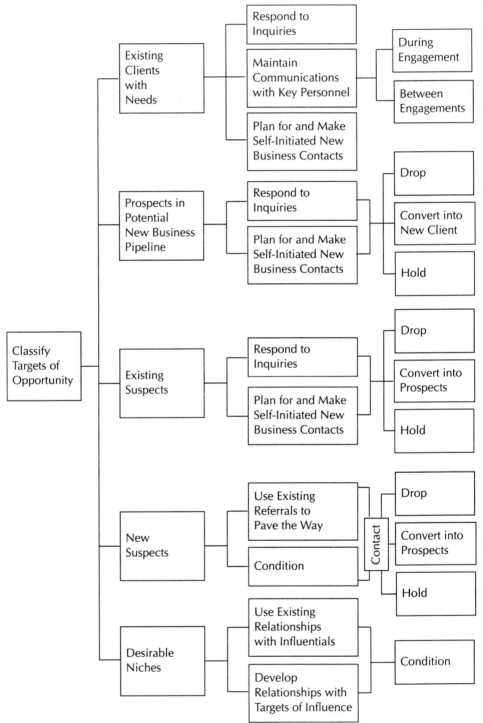

EXISTING CLIENTS WITH NEEDS—
OPPORTUNITY KNOCKS

Expanding services to existing "A"and "B" clients with needs for your services can be both enjoyable and profitable and is well within your comfort zone.

Once you have your list of targets of opportunity completed for the period, your next task is to develop and execute a contact program that involves bringing the need to the attention of the client's contact person.

Develop the Positive Point of View

The wrong frame of mind in laying the groundwork for expanding services to your clients is not to sell more services to your targets. Rather, proceed with the mind-set, "In what ways can I assist this client in doing better what that individual is in business to do?" This client-focused question helps avoid the pushing of your services and builds a sensitivity to being the means to a more favorable future. The how-tos of personal selling will be covered in Chapter 28, but for now your goal should be to enable clients to see that you have solutions to their most pressing needs and problems.

It Should Be Your Policy!

The rationale for bringing additional needs to the attention of the client should be established in the first new business meeting you have with a prospective client. For example, tell prospective clients, "It's our service philosophy to be alert to ways in which we can assist you in the conduct of your business. If during the course of the project we discover any area that we feel needs attention, we'll review our solution programs with you before we complete our work."

Build Marketing into the Engagement Process

A review of your marketing opportunities is particularly appropriate during five engagement phases:

1. *Pre-engagement planning.* Review your files on the client to determine which are the current hot-button needs.

2. *Entrance conference.* It's a good idea to review the Letter of Agreement with the client at this time. Mention that you'll be alert to ideas for improvement during the project and will share them at the end of the project.

3. *The engagement.* Be alert to the presence of needs beyond the scope of the current engagement. If you have staff on the engagement, insist that each prepare a client alert report (CAR) that defines an additional known or suspected need to be brought to the attention of the client. Be especially alert to symptoms of needs met by your successful engagements for other similar clients in this industry niche.

4. *End-of-engagement satisfaction meeting.* This is the selling meeting that too few professionals conduct. You begin the meeting by determining the level of client satisfaction with your services. If the reaction is favorable, you obtain referrals and leads and plant the seeds of future need. Properly handled, this meeting will extend into Phase 5.

5. *Post-engagement new business discussion.* During this sales meeting you review the need, identify your proposed solution, discuss procedures, and attempt to convince the client to proceed with your solution program.

CONVERTING YOUR PROSPECTIVE CLIENTS INTO NEW CLIENTS

For each prospect, what is your next step? You have two options:

- Send additional information designed to urge the potential client to proceed. Remind them of the benefits of proceeding, and the costs and consequences of not proceeding.

- Call your contact to see how the decision process is proceeding. A brief call consisting of an "I've been thinking about you and wonder how the decision process is coming along. Any news yet?" is sufficient, although it always pays to mention another benefit.

Eventually, if "Let's proceed" is not forthcoming, you have to make a decision. Do you drop this contact completely or just put them on hold for awhile? We recommend that you ask one more time if there is any chance of proceeding. If "no," Dick asks, "Was there something I missed during the proposal process? I really thought there was a fit between your need and my solution." Occasionally a prospect will suggest that the job had been wired (another favored consultant had the inside track) or the situation took a back seat to a more pressing need elsewhere in the organization.

FIGURE 9–2
Identifying Targets of Opportunity

1. Clients:
   A. With needs and the budget.
   B. With potential for upgrading:
      - "B" clients with potential for upgrading.
      - "C" clients who can be upgraded.
   C. From whom you can recover more by:
      - Getting more of the receivables.
      - Improving the engagement profitability due to rearrangement of the work and deliverable.
      - Upgrading a client whom you are giving a discount to retain his business.
2. Prospects in the pipeline to be converted during the marketing period.
3. Inquiries from nonclients.
4. Leads to follow up on during the marketing period.
5. Additional relationships to cultivate.
6. New niches for special attention.
7. Organizations comprised of targets of opportunity and targets of influence to which you can belong.

KEEP YOUR TARGETS' PIPELINE FULL AND FLOWING

Targets of opportunity have a relatively brief shelf life. Your goal is to constantly monitor the relationships and operations of your "A" clients and high-potential "B" clients for needs and corresponding opportunities to help them achieve their goals. (See Figure 9–2.) This is client-centered service at its finest and tends to generate profitable and recurring revenue.

In the next chapter we will examine the procedures to be followed in tracking your targets of attention.

CHAPTER 10

Managing Your Targets of Attention

This chapter discusses the analysis and actions you'll need to undertake to successfully manage your targets of attention. Attention is not equal to action, although, as you'll see, you will take action at critical junctures. We define attention as "observant or watchful consideration," combined with "civility and courtesy," all of which are essential attributes of a client-centered approach to marketing your services.

Upon conclusion of this chapter you will be able to:

☐ Identify and prioritize your current targets of attention.

☐ Determine the best forms of action with your targets of attention.

☐ Identify warning signals that indicate a strain or threat to the primary client-firm relationship.

☐ Employ a four-step client retention plan.

☐ Further leverage your precious business development time and resources.

☐ List actions to be taken in your personal marketing plan.

IDENTIFYING TARGETS OF ATTENTION

Who represents a target of attention to you? Among your clients, if you notice more than one of the following situations, it's a safe bet that this client merits your attention:

Revenues: Fees are either off, disputed, or in danger of not being collected.

Relationships: Relationships are showing signs of wear and tear—a client's staff is giving you or your staff difficulty, or communications are more troublesome.

Referrals: Referrals either are slowing or have stopped, or the quality of lead is diminishing.

Problems with clients: A client has a service concern or a fee complaint.

Profitability: You are not able to make your profit margins on the work for this client due to either your problems or the client's messing up or a combination of the two.

Leverage: You are investing too many resources for the results you are producing.

WORKING WITH YOUR TARGETS OF ATTENTION

The cliché "A stitch in time saves nine" really applies to your attention situations.

Your fundamental and continuing goal with your "A" clients and "B" clients with potential for upgrading should be to protect and retain the primary client-firm relationship. But situations arise that need to be dealt with. In today's increasingly competitive environment, it's realistic to expect that your most desirable clients are on the targets of attention or targets of opportunity lists of your most aggressive competitors. A light dose of paranoia is a good thing when your good clients are involved. In all cases of dissatisfaction or targeting, it is imperative that you initiate a client retention program.

A Policy from Which You Can Profit

Figure 10–1 provides a policy statement and checklist that permit you to monitor potential vulnerabilities with existing desirable clients

FIGURE 10–1
Policy and Checklist for Vulnerable Client Situations

In every relationship there is a vulnerability for things to go sour. In a service environment, vulnerable situations will always arise when service is substandard. While your organization aims at providing quality service, in certain situations, there may still be vulnerability. If the response to any of the following questions is positive, look at the impact it may have. Within the last 12 months:

		Yes	No
1.	Have we been late in meeting our commitments?	☐	☐
2.	Have we put new personnel on the engagement team?	☐	☐
3.	Have we had to replace any of the team members to satisfy the client?	☐	☐
4.	Have we given bad advice that has cost the client money?	☐	☐
5.	Have we taken key members of the client service team off the account?	☐	☐
6.	Have any key members of the client service team left the firm?	☐	☐
7.	Have we disagreed with the client on important issues?	☐	☐
8.	Has the client appointed a new chief executive?	☐	☐
9.	Has a new keyboard member been appointed?	☐	☐
10.	Does the CEO have a close relationship with an individual in another competitive firm?	☐	☐
11.	Is the client served by a bank or an attorney who does not respect us?	☐	☐
12.	Have we missed regular monthly contact with the client?	☐	☐
13.	Have we received limited or no calls for consultation?	☐	☐
14.	Is the client in financial trouble?	☐	☐
15.	Is there dissatisfaction on the client's part with our industry knowledge?	☐	☐
16.	Have we surprised the client lately with a significant issue?	☐	☐
17.	Have we reversed a position on advice given previously?	☐	☐
18.	Is the personal chemistry between any key member of the client service team and client management a problem?	☐	☐
19.	Is there a political situation brewing in the client organization?	☐	☐
20.	Do we have limited relationships?	☐	☐
21.	Are there effectively no relationships between firm and client?	☐	☐
22.	Does the client have a history of rotating service providers?	☐	☐
23.	Has the client acquired a company or business served by another firm that offers similar services?	☐	☐
24.	Is the client's parent company served by others who compete with us?	☐	☐
25.	Has the client been recently acquired by a company with other service providers?	☐	☐
26.	Is the client vulnerable to takeover?	☐	☐

Source: Adapted from Dick Connor, *Increasing Revenue from Your Clients* (New York: John Wiley & Sons, 1989), p. 203.

and to remain alert to early warning signals that threaten the relationship. This checklist should be completed by you and others serving your best clients at the end of *every* engagement.

Client Retention Planning

The intent of client retention planning is to spot situations where you need to take steps quickly and surely to secure the relationship with the client. Client retention planning involves analysis, planning, action, and follow-up. One without the others is insufficient.

1. *Analysis* requires an accurate, client-centered description of the situation: "Who is involved in what ways?" "What specifically has been observed/heard/done that suggests dissatisfaction?" "How urgent is it that this situation be handled?"

2. *Planning* involves assigning responsibility; allocating resources such as information, budget, and time; and developing a time-phased action program.

3. *Action* is the execution of the planned activities.

4. *Follow-up* is the act of checking today's reality against the situation defined earlier.

Congratulations! You have completed an important step in the development of your client-centered marketing program. In the next chapter we'll discuss the procedures to be followed in working with your targets of influence.

CHAPTER 11

Managing Your Targets of Influence

This chapter extends the information about nonclient influentials introduced in Chapter 6. Targets of influence refer to the additional relationships you seek to develop with targeted attorneys, bankers, editors, executive directors of industry associations, community leaders, and others who can provide you with leads or vouch for your ability to serve.

Upon conclusion of this chapter you will be able to:

☐ Identify additional nonclient influentials with whom you want to develop a referral-driven relationship.

☐ Create and maintain favorable visibility with them.

☐ Develop relationships with them based on mutual interest.

☐ Further develop the relationship into a referral-producing relationship.

☐ Develop the know-how to avoid receiving undesirable referrals.

IDENTIFYING ADDITIONAL TARGETS OF INFLUENCE

Your task is to identify the names of additional nonclients who influence and impact your targeted industry–market niches. In addition to the sources listed in Chapter 6, consider these sources:

- Clients who are served by other noncompeting consultants they respect.

- Other current nonclient referral sources who are interested in expanding their network of relationships with others they respect.

- Announcements of new noncompeting firms who may be future reciprocal referral relationships, such as attorneys and accountants.

CREATE A FAVORABLE VISIBILITY WITH TARGETS OF INFLUENCE

Creating an initial and continuing favorable visibility requires planning followed by action. After you develop your list of names, determine where these targets congregate, make it a point to attend the functions they attend, and arrange introductions through mutual friends or sponsors of the events.

One of Dick's public relations clients developed a referral relationship with a highly influential source. During a visit to London, the client made a cold-call, drop-in contact, telling the target, "Since we are both in the same field, and I happened to be in town, I thought it made sense to say hello and develop a relationship." Within a year, this London source arranged for Dick's client to make a keynote address to a highly influential group of potential contacts for the client's specialized type of services in London.

In lieu of face-to-face contact, sending a note of congratulations for an award or event in which the possible contact was featured is appropriate. We both receive many contacts from others serving our types of clients after they have read our books. Some of these noncompetitive contacts have developed into good referral sources.

DEVELOP A RELATIONSHIP BASED ON MUTUAL INTEREST

We've found it useful to take the initiative when developing a long-term relationship with a target. We ask, "Does it make sense for us to move into a mutually beneficial referral mode? Serving the . . . niche is one of my current goals, and I'd be glad to think through with you how we can assist each other in using our relationship and reputation in getting leads." At this point we show our preferred prospective client profile. (See Figure 11–1.) We review the criteria we have for desirable clients and, also, what constitutes our knock out factors.

What we are really doing is reviewing our criteria for classifying "A" clients (discussed in Chapter 4). Being up-front eliminates a lot of misunderstanding between you and the new source and prevents many potentially expensive problems in serving marginal clients you felt you had to take to keep the relationship alive with the new referral source.

A *word of warning:* Don't move too quickly in your goal of exchanging your databases with each other. We do this only after we've checked

FIGURE 11–1
Preferred Prospective Client Profile

Positive Characteristics of "A" Clients

1._____

2._____

3._____

4._____

5._____

6._____

7._____

8._____

9._____

Knock Out Factors—"C" and "D" Clients

1._____

2._____

3._____

4._____

5._____

6._____

7._____

out the ethics, reliability, and staying power of the possible new referral source.

DEVELOPING A REFERRAL-PRODUCING RELATIONSHIP

A referral-producing relationship simply grows out of the previous steps. One of you provides the other with the name(s) of clients they are comfortable in having you contact or, better still, in arranging for introductions.

Make an Early Decision about the New Relationship

Give the new relationship a six- to nine-month trial. If the names are flowing and the contacts agree to meet with you, fine. If you experience undue difficulty in getting in to see the leads, once again review your preferred prospective client profile with the source to be certain you are in harmony and can attract desirable new clients.

List the names of targeted contacts under the targets of influence section on your personal marketing plan.

In the next chapter we will examine the procedure to be followed in selection of an industry for special attention.

CHAPTER 12

Selecting an Industry for Special Attention

Unless your marketing comfort zone is large enough to handle the inevitable rejections that accompany wide-angle, horizontal prospecting, you'll find that selecting an industry–market niche for analysis and action is a much easier way to conduct your prospecting activities. In other words, you make a strategic decision to segment your business by industries (starting with one industry) as the basis of your specialization. An accounting firm that primarily serves health-care agencies would be an example of this.

The key to fairly predictable, significant growth is to be "somebody special to a special group of bodies." You need to be perceived as being different and better. This chapter will help you designate an industry for analysis and action as the first step in selecting a targeted industry–market niche.

Upon completing the chapter you will be able to answer the following questions:

☐ Why is the selection of an industry for subsequent niching a strategic decision?

☐ What's the simplest way to select your industries for special attention?

☐ Where do you find industry data sources?

☐ What criteria are used in selection of the industry?

KEY DEFINITIONS REVISITED

So that we are talking the same game, here's a review of some working definitions:

Industry refers to your clients and prospects who are sellers of similar products and services to their customers and prospects—for example, bankers, hospitals, or tire manufacturers.

Market refers to your industry-specific clients and prospects who are buyers for your need-satisfying, value-adding solutions.

Niche is used as an abbreviation for industry–market niche.

Strategic decisions "bet the farm." They involve major resource commitments that determine where and how a business competes against other firms vying for the same clients.

You can't be all things to all people, and you certainly can't be all things to all clients. Choosing an industry–market niche is one of the most important strategic decisions you can make regarding the long-term viability of your practice. The key is to direct your attention to industry–market niche(s) where you can most readily serve and most prosperously penetrate. As we acknowledged earlier, it's likely that you face the challenge of getting new clients with limited resources. Even if you had unlimited resources, you still would want to allocate them wisely and appropriately.

In assessing industries, ask yourself, "Do I rechoose my current primary industries?" If not, examine secondary industries that warrant further attention. The industries that you primarily serve need to be ones that constitute a relatively large percentage of your total revenue. Your secondary industries are clients who represent a smaller, though significant percentage of your total revenue and whom you can readily serve.

THE SELECTION PROCESS

Ideally, you serve at least two industry–market niches that have counterbalancing business-activity cycles. This enables you to level your workload and helps offset unexpected variances. For example, Dick serves churches during the November-to-April busy season encountered by CPAs. Jeff speaks to accounting and banking groups in the summer months, after the tax season and when loan activity is somewhat slower.

Choosing an industry or industries on which to concentrate is an evolutionary process. It starts with examining appropriate industries (by four-digit SIC code number). It ends with getting work with new clients that can be done in a realistic time frame at a price affordable to the client and profitable to you.

As a rule of thumb, you want to select a relatively stable niche not dominated by one or more of your competitors. It is helpful if your technological capability is perceived as state-of-the-art at the least—leading-edge is preferable. If you already have some desirable clients in the niche you ultimately select, or if you have relationships with niche influentials, these are certainly plus factors. Likewise, if you or your staff is experienced and enjoys working in the niche, this is a big plus. Here are four considerations:

1. *Identify the industries you serve at present.* This step is easy to complete if you have classified your clients by the industry in which they serve and compete. If you have not yet done this analysis, please return to Chapter 4 and follow the suggestions.

2. *Determine your primary and secondary industries.* A primary industry is one that constitutes a relatively large percentage of your total revenue. A secondary industry is one that currently generates a relatively small percentage of total revenue.

3. *Estimate the potential for growth.* In choosing your industry, it is important to estimate the potential for future growth among primary- and secondary-industry candidates. Past trends are one thing. Is the industry growing at a rapid pace, or is it relatively stable? If the estimates for potential growth within a primary industry indicate slow or no growth, either abandon further action within that industry, or maintain your current level of effort in serving it.

   You can elect to continue to accept all inquiries regarding your services from firms in an industry, even if the potential for industry growth is low. You may even choose to follow through if you are in a survival mode. Your goal, however, is to focus on primary industries that have a high potential growth estimate. Examining these industries in relationship to their geographic representation, including proximity and accessibility, aids in identifying niche candidates.

4. *Does it fit?* Were you to select this particular niche, what specific experience do you have in serving it? What resources would you use, including existing relationships, industry data, or other inside information or competitive advantages? What is your current image and reputation within the niche? What promotion techniques could you use to stimulate interest? Are the organizations and memberships you currently maintain sufficient for meeting prospects and nonclient influentials? Or, would you have to join other organizations?

Is your niche dominated by a few companies? Are the needs of typical prospective clients in this industry such that any work you do for them will be challenging to your staff and transferable to other clients?

Many other criteria could be used for selecting your niche. Over the years, we have found that the following are among the most important:

- The number of existing key and "A" clients in the niche.

- The nature of your competition.

- The interests of you and your key staff.

- The ability to transfer your technology developed from serving clients in a related industry.

- The number and strengths of your nonclient influentials.

- The estimated costs of identifying and contacting the targets.

- The costs of developing a sufficient insider's understanding.

- The costs of developing appropriate technologies required to provide support services.

- The support and cooperation of partners with relative experience in the niche.

Data Sources

One reliable source of information for estimating potential growth is *Predicasts*, by F&S Publications. It forecasts growth of all industries by SIC number. *Predicasts* is a useful tool in accelerating your understanding of the growth and future direction of your niche. *Predicasts* is available in the business reference section of any major city library, university library, or federal-government-related library.

Another excellent source is the trade association serving the industry. Industry and professional trade associations contain a wealth of information regarding trends in their respective industries. Associations can provide industry trend information, surveys, publications, and many other services.

Association directories can be found at any library and offer the names, addresses, and telephone numbers of industry, trade, and professional associations. Two directories in particular—Gale's *Encyclopedia of Associations* and *National Trade and Professional Associations of the United States*—collectively offer more than 10,000 association listings.

The U.S. Department of Commerce produces the *United States Industrial Outlook*, which traces the growth of 200 industries and provides five-year forecasts for each industry. This publication is available by mail. Write to:

> Superintendent of Documents
> U.S. Government Printing Office
> Washington, DC 20401

Determine the Number of the Industry's Players in Your Market Area

In obtaining relevant information to help you make your final decision regarding which niche(s) to select, leave no stone unturned. Among the basic data you need are the raw numbers of prospects within the niches you're examining. The best source of SIC and business segmentation data can be obtained from the aforementioned American Business Information. Write to them for a free copy of their "Lists of 10 Million Businesses." When you receive this informative publication you'll see at a glance the number of organizations listed by SIC within each state. Again, their address is:

> American Business Information
> 5711 South 86th Circle
> P.O. Box 27347
> Omaha, NE 68127

Make the Go/No-Go Decision

By now, you have done your analysis and determined the areas in which you want to specialize. Hopefully, you have identified something different and better about your services so that you can attract those "special bodies." Ultimately, you reach the moment of truth, the time in which a go/no-go decision needs to be made regarding the industry–market niche you have been analyzing. It would be nice to have a simple formula to make the most appropriate choice. Unfortunately, there isn't one; at least, we haven't encountered it.

After all of your study and analysis, niche decisions are of a qualitative, subjective nature. Your decision to go with a particular niche has to feel right.

Making the niche decision involves taking calculated risks. The analysis you have undertaken provides you with more informed decision-making capabilities. You also need to have confidence in your capabilities to enter and successfully penetrate the niche that you define. This will involve dropping what does not fit unless it is needed for short-term survival.

If you have any doubts about selecting a particular niche, don't select it. A bad choice can be costly. Your decision influences strategic practice decisions.

As with any decision, there are always costs involved. Perhaps the hardest decision to make is to abandon a niche that you had previously penetrated. After all, you have already invested time and resources. Abandoning the niche would force you to acknowledge time and money lost and engender feelings of guilt and second-guessing.

A final "gut check" is in order: The niche that you choose has to be one in which you are willing to commit and invest your time, technology, and resources, so that you can stand out from the herd.

When you have completed the industry selection process, you will be ready to handle the industry analysis steps that are discussed in the next chapter.

PART FOUR
An Insider's Understanding

CHAPTER 13

Developing an Insider's Understanding of the Industry

Now that you have selected an industry for special attention, it's time to apply that attention to developing what we call an insider's understanding. An insider's understanding refers to your in-depth knowledge of how the niche works, what it takes to make a profit and compete successfully, and the structure and dynamics of the industry and market(s) within the niche.

Upon completing this chapter you will be able to answer the following questions:

☐ Where do you find industry data sources?

☐ How do you determine the structure of the industry?

☐ What does the term *nature of the industry* mean?

☐ What are an industry's dynamics, and how do you determine them?

☐ What is the best way to summarize your industry information?

FINDING INDUSTRY DATA SOURCES

Getting smart about an industry is not difficult in today's information society. There is no shortage of data sources. The issue is how to best limit and leverage the amount of data you need to develop. To find industry data:

1. *Learn to use your local libraries.* Introduce yourself to the reference librarian and say that you want to get smart about an industry.

2. *Contact the trade/professional association(s) serving the industry.* Many associations publish studies regarding the growth potential of the industry as well as information about pending legislation that may impact the member organizations. The aforementioned Gale's *Encyclopedia of Associations* and *National Trade and Professional Associations of the United States* collectively offer more than 10,000 association listings.

3. *Talk with your best clients.* Determine what your clients read and to what sources they refer.

4. *Use on-line digital sources.* Commercial sources such as CompuServe and Prodigy can be valuable tools for uncovering industry-specific information. The Internet offers a world of knowledge when you learn how to access its thousands of databases and millions of sites.

5. *Attend industry trade shows and conferences.* Annual industry conferences often deal with important issues and needs. Even if you don't attend the conference, develop a list of names of presenters and add them to your industry database. Later on you can treat these people as targets of influence and begin developing a relationship with them.

DETERMINING AN INDUSTRY'S STRUCTURE

Structure refers to the way the industry is organized and the requirements to be successful. Knowledge of an industry's structure provides you with essential information for building an insider's reputation. To determine an industry's structure:

1. Determine the size and composition of the industry. How large is the industry? Refer to one or more of these sources: *The U.S. Industrial Outlook, Forbes, Business Week, Industry News*, and the trade or professional association serving the industry. What is the composition of the industry?

   - Big market leaders accounting for a major percentage of sales;
   - Some big firms, many of moderate size, and many small firms; or
   - Majority of small, low-market-share firms.

2. What segmentation is occurring? Who is merging with whom and why?

3. What stage of growth is the industry in? Embryonic, growth, maturity, or aging stage?

4. What has been the rate of growth?

5. What expansion strategies are in play?

6. Are the industry boundaries stable or blurring?

7. Who are the key players in the industry?

   - Association executives.
   - Editors of publications serving the industry.
   - Industry influentials such as gurus, analysts, and so on.
   - Organizations that serve the industry.
   - Organizations that regulate the industry.

DETERMINING THE NATURE OF THE INDUSTRY

The *nature of the industry* refers to the processes used in the manufacture/production or delivery of the service or product. Here are some key questions:

1. What production technology is used?

   - Producing one at a time—consulting engagements, Wendy's hamburgers, audits, wills.

- Batching (producing small quantities of similar products held in inventory)—McDonald's, Pizza Hut.

- Mass production—automotive industry is a good example.

- Process flow—chemicals, steel, and so on.

2. What are the critical success factors (CSFs) for the industry? Every industry has CSF or performance areas where things must go correctly for a business to flourish, given its location, stage of growth, mission, and growth strategies. To identify the CSFs in an industry, refer to Figure 13–1.

As a result of your search you may also begin to have a feel for the industry's cost structure. Are the primary costs largely fixed or variable? What key business functions incur the major portion of costs? Within the key business functions, where do the major costs reside?

FIGURE 13–1
Sources of Industry Critical Success Factors (CSFs) Information

Critical success factors usually consist of three to eight performance factors that the winners in the industry typically employ.

To identify the CSFs in an industry:

1. Ask your clients about the winners in the industry. Ask them, "What factors are so fundamental to success in the industry that you've got to get them right?" "What performance indicators do you monitor and why?" "What ratios do you prepare and monitor?"

2. Read company annual reports of listed organizations. Identify the factors they discuss that both aided and limited them during the year.

3. Talk with stockbrokers who specialize in the industry. Look for the names of brokers mentioned in the "On the Street" column in the *Wall Street Journal* or in articles in *Financial Management, Barron's,* and *Forbes.*

4. Study the prospectuses issued by companies in the industry that seek to go public. Pay particular attention to risk factors spelled out in the analysis section.

5. Talk with industry gurus. You can find their names in the publications you review.

DETERMINING THE INDUSTRY'S DYNAMICS

The term *dynamics* refers to the changes, trends, forces, and legislature affecting the players in the industry. To determine an industry's dynamics:

1. Identify the trends that are evident and emerging. Consider the major directions and paths the industry is taking, such as mergers, strategic alliances, and outsourcing.

2. Determine what is occurring in the technological environment. This environment is characterized by an explosion in information technology and computer-driven innovations, the re-engineering process reinvention movement, and increased regulation of technological change. Consider at least these questions:

   - What new product developments are occurring?

   - What new materials, manufacturing, or production processes are being developed?

   - What is the impact of information technology?

   - What future changes in the industry's core technology are being discussed?

   - What political and regulatory forces are in play? Check with your clients, and speak with accountants and attorneys who serve the industry. Use on-line information sources to get information about current and pending regulation.

Refer to Figure 13–2, A Checklist of Industry Data Sources, to see if it triggers additional information.

From your review of industry data sources, you can begin to understand more about the buying factors in play. For example, what is the length of the buying cycle? What triggers the buying decision? What are the titles of those in the decision-making unit (DMU)?

SUMMARIZING YOUR INDUSTRY INFORMATION

We suggest that you organize your industry data both in your database and in an industry notebook. Organize your data using these sections:

FIGURE 13–2
A Checklist of Industry Data Sources

Directories
- *Findex*
- *Million Dollar Directory*
- *News Front: Reports on 30,000 Leading U.S. Corporations*
- *North American Register of Business and Industry*
- *Standard Directory of Advertisers*
- *Thomas Register of American Manufacturers*
- *Corporate 1000*
- *Standard & Poor's Register of Corporations, Directors and Executives*
- *Dun's Middle Market Directory*

Magazines
- *Magazine Industry Marketplace*
- *Magazine Index*
- *Readers' Guide to Periodical Literature*
- *Business Week*
- *Financial World*
- *Fortune*
- *Industry Week*

Newspapers
- *New York Times Index*
- *Wall Street Journal Index*

Newsletters
- *Oxbridge Directory of Newsletters*
- *National Trade and Professional Associations of the United States (NTPA)*
- *Newsletter Yearbook Directory*

Research Studies
- *Findex*
- *Predicasts*

On-Line Sources
- *Disclosure II*
- *Investext*
- *Magazine Index*
- *Management Contents*
- *National Newspaper Index*

1. SIC code and industry description.
2. Industry structure.
3. Industry dynamics in play.
4. Your experience in serving players in the industry.
5. Key intelligence, such as publications, associations, and legislative matters.

In the next chapter we'll discuss the actions and steps involved in developing an insider's understanding of the niche's market.

CHAPTER 14

Developing an Insider's Understanding of Your Niche's Market

You have selected an industry for special attention and developed an insider's understanding of the niche's industry. You're on the path to developing "client smarts." In this chapter you will complete your quest for an insider's understanding by developing smarts about the markets in which your clients and prospects reside and operate.

A market refers to your industry-specific clients and prospects who are in your geographic market area and in cyberspace and who are buyers for your type of services. The term *market* can also be thought of as a set of unfilled needs and wants held by targets of opportunity that can be met by the use of resources available to you. A market and the revenue derived from it are the purpose of your being in business. A niche's market also includes the competitive individuals and organizations vying for business you are seeking.

Developing an insider's understanding is essential to get in sync with targeted buyers. In general, markets tend be shrinking and fragmenting. Many markets are characterized by slow growth and fierce competition. Your challenge as a client-centered marketer is to recognize and adjust to market conditions that drive and impact the business strategies of all the players in the market.

Upon completing this chapter you will be able to answer the following questions:

☐ Where do you find market data sources?

☐ How do you determine the market's structure?

☐ How do you identify the market-affecting forces in play?

☐ What is the best way to summarize your market information?

FINDING MARKET DATA SOURCES

Developing an understanding of the niche's market is easy given the amount of information readily available to you. The issue is how to best limit and leverage the amount of data you need to acquire and analyze. To find essential market data:

1. *Learn to use your local libraries.* Introduce yourself to the reference librarian and say that you want to get smart about your served markets. Show the ZIP codes included.

   ■ Ask what services and materials are available within the library, or can be obtained from other sources such as interlibrary loan systems.

   ■ Determine the market-specific directories, newsletters, magazines, and associations serving the market.

   ■ Determine business publications that research and depict market conditions.

   ■ Find the reference shelf. Go to section 658 (the business subject area based on the Dewey decimal classification system employed by most American libraries). Determine the directories and publications available dealing with your market.

2. Contact the trade/professional association(s) serving the market. Many associations publish studies regarding the growth potential of the market.

3. Talk with your best clients to determine what market sources they use.

4. Use on-line digital sources.

5. Attend trade shows and conferences conducted in the market.

DETERMINING THE MARKET'S STRUCTURE

A niche's market is a collection of industry players, your clients, prospects, and suspects that reside in your practice area, and the competitive individuals and organizations vying for their business. To determine the market's geographical structure:

1. Analyze the ZIPs, including:

   - Demographic makeup. CompuServe's *Neighborhood Report* provides a summary of the demographic makeup of every U.S. ZIP code.

   - Sales and revenue data. *Sales Management & Marketing* magazine publishes an annual summary of buying power by geographic areas. Your local chamber of commerce can provide you with this information for the immediate area.

2. Identify the industry players in the ZIPs:

   - List the names of clients you serve and have served.

   - List the names of prospects in your new-business pipeline.

   - Describe the nature of client and prospect organizations: headquarters, branch, division, local.

   - List the names of niche influentials such as gurus, media personalities, analysts, and editors of market-specific publications whom you know or need to know.

   - List the names and specialties of others who compete for your targets of opportunity. Refer to Figure 14–1.

DETERMINING THE MARKET-AFFECTING FORCES IN PLAY

External market-affecting factors such as slow growth, increased competition, and so forth are important to understand and monitor. To determine the market-affecting forces, consider:

1. External environmental forces: economic, social, technological, political.

2. Trends such as downsizing and globalization: Develop a finite list of key variables.

FIGURE 14–1
Sizing Up the Individual Players in the Market

1. Who are the players?
   - Clients.
   - Prospects.
   - Suspects.
   - Competitors.
   - Influentials.
2. How do the players compete? Key questions include:
   A. How many individuals and organizations compete with me?
   B. Are there logical groups of competitors?

ZIPs:	*Specializations:*
■ International.	■ Services/products.
■ National.	■ SICs.
■ Regional.	■ Technologies.
■ Local.	

   C. Why is each competitor here?
      - Economic reasons.
      - Love of the activity.
      - As a base to learn technology to migrate.
      - Other(s).
   D. Where and how do they compete?
      - Business arenas: marketing, products, financial R&D.
      - Weapons: product characteristics, pricing, promotion.
   E. At what level does each operate?
      - Product versus product.
      - Business strategy versus business strategy: visibility, pricing.
      - Firm versus firm: IBM versus Apple.
   F. What strategic groups have formed? (A strategic group is a set of individuals and organizations in an industry that follows similar strategies in an attempt to set the rules of the competitive game.)
      - Determine the organizations that serve the market, such as trade association(s), educational enterprises, noncompeting consultants and the like, and research organizations, such as Frost & Sullivan Market Intelligence and Standard & Poor's.
      - Determine the organizations that regulate the market, such as federal and state bureaucracies, and professional societies, such as the American Institute of Certified Public Accountants and the American Bar Association.

3. Existing economic conditions: Are they strong, fair, weak?

4. The nature and extent of competition: Review competitor information—brochures, statements of capability, copies of proposals, news clippings, and so on.

5. The buying process for your types of services: Determine the decision-making unit (DMU) of the client or prospect organization. These are the individuals who are involved in the decision to purchase and use your proposed need solution. Within each client you want to determine the names and titles of the DMU players. Also consider:

   ■ Expectations: The desires, hopes, and wishes of the key DMU players must be understood and managed. Expectations at the base level have changed—clients expect more at less cost or at no additional cost. Expectations at the dynamic, daily level are fluid and in constant change.

   ■ Length of the sales cycle: The average elapsed time from initial contact to contract approval.

   ■ Buying factors: The frequency of purchase, trigger for making the buying decision, and the core buying motive—is it for security, profit, growth, survival, or other reasons?

SUMMARIZING AND ORGANIZING YOUR MARKET DATA

To distill your knowledge of the niche's market, prepare the work sheet shown in Figure 14–2. In section 1a, ask yourself, "What are the concerns of clients in this niche?" Then, list those concerns in the space provided. If your targeted niche is the construction industry, SIC number 1611, your answers might include "cost control," "timely reporting in control of multiple jobs," and "too much overhead."

For item 1b, answer the question, "What are the problems these clients face?" Even if you can't help the clients with these problems, you want to know what they are because it gives you more empathy and opportunities for meaningful discussion. If your clients are in the retail office supply business, SIC number 5943, your answers might include "compliance with the new tax laws," "employee pilferage," and "price instability among suppliers."

In 1c, ask, "What are clients in the niche vitally interested in that I

FIGURE 14–2
An Insider's Market Analysis

Niche: _____
               (SIC No. and Description)   (Date)

---

1. Clients in this niche:

   a. Are concerned with: _____

      Are concerned about: _____

   b. Are forced to do: _____

      Are forced to have: _____

   c. Would like to do: _____

      Would like to have: _____

   d. Are influenced by whom: _____

      Are influenced by what: _____

2. Current hot buttons include: _____

   _____

3. Industry-success factors include: _____

   _____

4. Information sources include: _____

   Directories: _____

   Publications: _____

   Organizations: _____

   Associations: _____

---

can assist them in doing or obtaining?" If your client is an EDP-systems installer, the answer might be "to obtain cost-plus contracts versus fixed-fee," "to maintain a smooth cash flow," and "to develop more confident junior staff who can service client needs." Practically speaking, your ability to answer 1c-type questions equates with your ability to identify new business opportunities for your firm.

In 1d, ask, "Who and what positively influence clients in this niche?" If your clients are real estate agents, for example, the answers might include "banks and savings and loan institutions," "corporate relocation officers," and "availability and condition of existing housing."

Item 2 asks for the current hot buttons in the niche. Hot buttons consist of any topics, issues, or trends of a contemporary and keen interest to prospects within this niche. If your clients are members of the airline industry, for example, current hot buttons might include "shortages in air traffic controllers," "terrorism," "discount airfares," and "frequent flyer programs."

For number 3, determine as many of the industry-success factors as you can for this niche. If your clients are industrial launderers, SIC number 7212, this list might include "efficient use of energy," "maintaining cost control over supplies," "eliminating waste," "passing EPA and OSHA inspections," "securing corporate accounts," "maintaining schedules," and "customer deadlines."

For number 4, list the best directories for this niche, the ones that give you insider information. If your niche consists of one-to-five-person public-accounting firms, SIC number 8721, you would certainly want to list the directory of the National Society of Public Accountants, with more than 18,000 members. Next, list the publications read by your clients and prospects in the niche. If your target consists of design and product engineers, SIC number 8711, publications of interest would include *Design News*, *Machine Design*, *Product Design and Development*, and *Product Engineering*. The subscriber lists of these publications are for sale; hence, you can use them to identify targets of opportunity in your market area.

Next, identify the organizations and associations to which your clients and prospects belong. If your clients consist of machine shops, SIC number 3599, these organizations might include the National Association of Manufacturers, the National Federation of Independent Businesses, and the U.S. Department of Commerce.

In the next chapter we will discuss how to identify the niche's needs that you will select to serve through the use of value-adding solutions.

CHAPTER 15

Selecting Needs You Can Meet with Available Resources

This is an important chapter for you. A client-centered marketer monitors the new and emerging needs of clients in the niche and endeavors to offer new solutions and/or products, and improved versions of current products and solutions.

Need identification, fulfillment, and satisfaction, not the selling of a service or product, is the obsession and primary focus of the client-centered marketer. During the process of building your insider's understanding, you were alert to needs in the niche that, quite possibly, you *could* meet with the resources now available to you.

In this chapter we are going to describe a need selection system that is both simple and powerful because it quickly narrows down the most likely needs for you to select for subsequent value-adding solution actions.

In this chapter you will:

☐ Prepare a need-solution candidate matrix.

☐ Identify candidates.

☐ Prepare a customized set of solution criteria for your situation.

☐ Identify the likely needs for which you can and should prepare a value-adding solution.

THE NEED-SOLUTION CANDIDATE MATRIX

Preparing the Need-Solution Candidate Matrix

Please refer to Figure 15–1 to see the kinds of information you'll be entering in your need-solution candidate matrix. Note that there are three broad categories of needs: mission-critical, market-critical, and other needs.

Mission-critical needs are internal and deal with reducing fixed costs, reducing variable costs, improving the mix of service and/or product offerings, and the like. Some clients refer to these as critical success factors (CSFs), which were discussed earlier in Chapter 13. Regardless of what they are called, they represent make-or-break performance areas for the client.

FIGURE 15–1
Need-Solution Candidate Matrix

Date Prepared: __/__/__

1	2	3	4
Niche Needs	Able to Meet with Resources Available to Us	Best Candidates for Solution Building	Priority
Mission-critical:			
Market-critical:			
Other:			

Market-critical needs are external in focus and deal with improving prices, reducing returns, recognition as being different and/or better (D&B), relationships with infrastructure, image, reputation, and the like.

Other needs are those that don't fit the two basic categories, but that you feel may be important enough to warrant your attention.

In preparation for completing the matrix, please return to Figure 13–1, Sources of CSF Information, and Figure 14–2, Insider's Market Analysis. Scan the two figures and list the needs that come to mind in the appropriate sections in Figure 15–1 (Column 1).

Determining Your Evaluative Criteria

After you have listed the niche needs in Column 1, put a check mark in Column 2 after those you are able to meet with the resources available to you. Your next critical step is to prepare the list of criteria you will use in selecting candidate needs for solution building. Start by considering these criteria:

- Multiple clients/prospects have this need.
- The need is important now.
- There is high market attractiveness.
- There is high visibility.
- Need has large value to client.
- We will be able to produce early visible results.
- Solution has a short payout period.
- Solution is easiest to deliver with our resources.
- Solution building will involve our best people.
- Our solution program technology is at least on the trailing edge of the leading edge.

Feel free to remove those items that don't fit, and add others that better meet your situation. Place a check mark in Column 3 after the needs for which solution building would meet *all* or *most* of your criteria.

Establishing Final Priority Rankings

Using the revised set of criteria, establish your final priority rankings. Remember, the needs for which you set priorities are the same ones for which you will prepare value-adding solutions. Place a number indicating your priority for solution building in Column 4 opposite the candidate list.

TIME AGAIN FOR A GUT CHECK

Selecting needs for which you will build value-adding solutions is another strategic decision that involves making a substantial investment of time, money, and expensive resources. Take the time now for another gut check—can you live with the decision long-term, and are you committed to seeing the job through?

If Yes, congratulations—you have winnowed down the needs of the niche into a list of needs for which you're going to build solutions. We turn now to handling this task.

PART FIVE
Serving the Niche

CHAPTER 16

Building Marketing into the Fabric of the Firm

In Chapter 1 we mentioned that elevating marketing to major firm status was fundamental to the success of your firm. Indeed, not to do so is a key marketing mistake. Dr. Peter Drucker believes that, "Marketing is so basic that it cannot be considered a separate function . . . on a par with others such as manufacturing or personnel. . . . it is, first, a central dimension of the entire business. It is the whole business seen from the point of view of its final result, that is, from the customer's point of view." (*Management: Tasks, Responsibilities, Practices*, page 63).

So, how do you make marketing part of the fabric of your firm? Read on. After completing this chapter and absorbing the ideas, you will be able to:

☐ Justify your strategic decision to make client-centered marketing the central dimension of your entire business.

☐ Build marketing into your firm's engagement/project procedures.

☐ Build marketing into the firm's appraisal and development process.

☐ Build client-centered marketing tools that enable you to leverage your time and niche-specific information.

RAISING MARKETING TO MISSION-CRITICAL STATUS

"Mission-critical" means that a mistake can be detrimental to the success of a firm. There is too much riding on the outcome. So, too, in your firm, you must ensure that everyone associated with your business recognizes and is committed to making client-centered marketing and all that it implies a vital core function and dimension of "the way things are done around here."

BUILDING MARKETING INTO ENGAGEMENT/ PROJECT PROCEDURES

Your client-centered marketing program should be built into your engagement process. This is a five-stage process that is relatively simple to achieve.

Pre-engagement Planning

During the pre-engagement planning phase, you review relevant correspondence, client service plans, and client alert reports to examine new business leads. Some of these leads might require additional work and research, which should be incorporated into your pre-engagement planning. Client service plans and client alert reports will be discussed later in the chapter.

Entrance Conference

The core strategy in the conference is to manage the expectations of those involved. At this conference, you meet with the client to begin the engagement, and you review the job performance criteria that define the scope of the engagement. In identifying client expectations, it is important to be as specific as possible so that the scope of the engagement is not arbitrarily expanded. Any significant additional responsibilities you take on should result in a modification of your initial agreement letter.

Conduct of the Engagement

While every engagement will be different, there are several essential factors to keep in mind and to manage:

Managing your visibility. Your goal is to manage your visibility in such a way that the client feels confident of getting full value from your services. Observe the work hours of the location and, be there at the start of the workday. Make opportunities to encounter key people in the parking lot, lunchrooms, and other such locations.

Solution design and development. Your goal is to design a solution that will be installed; then, client satisfaction is assured when what you do works. Dick's boss at Booz, Allen & Hamilton often told him, "I'll take one hundred percent acceptance of a fifty percent idea anytime. I'll fire anyone who only gets fifty percent acceptance of any idea, no matter how good it is. If the client doesn't experience movement, we've failed!"

Solution installation. Preselling your solution to key client personnel and preparing the site for the installation are the hallmarks of the client-centered marketing professional.

Engagement Wrap-Up

At the conclusion of the engagement, you conduct a client satisfaction meeting where you determine the level of client satisfaction with your services, solicit referrals, and plant the seeds of future need. When future (or additional) client needs are ready for discussion, the client satisfaction meeting will often extend into a postengagement conference, where you propose additional services, identify solutions to client problems, and start the entire process rolling once again.

After-the-Sale Support

Too many busy marketers love and leave a client after the initial engagement has been completed. After-the-sale, support is the single most important factor in building a relationship that will outlast occasional mistakes and in enabling you to reach into the organization as needed.

THE POLICY STATEMENT

The rationale for bringing additional needs to the attention of a client should be established in the first new business meeting you have with a prospective client. When you talk about firm policy in that meeting, you can inform the client that your firm's policy is to bring items of interest that you discover to the client's attention.

BUILDING MARKETING INTO THE APPRAISAL AND DEVELOPMENT PROCESS

There are two fundamental steps to be taken:

1. Setting marketing responsibilities by level of staff.
2. Rewarding adherence to the requirements.

Setting Marketing Responsibilities by Level of Staff

The TQM movement proved a point that was widely held: "Unless you measure an activity you will probably not have consistent performance."

Measurement begins with specificity. Figure 16–1 shows the marketing responsibilities by staff level that Dick developed for a major accounting firm. Note that several of the marketing responsibilities were shared by several levels, but at a different level/scope of responsibility.

Rewarding Adherence to the Requirements

The old management truism of "Go along to get along" holds true in building marketing into the fabric of the firm. Rewarding staff who willingly participate in the marketing process should not be left to chance. In the next chapter you'll be told to tie promotion and career development to meeting responsibilities. For now, it's enough to remind you to set in place a specific reward structure. The structure will likely contain both financial and other nonfinancial perks such as paid sponsorship in organizations, payment of tuition for courses of mutual interest to the firm and the individual and the like.

PREPARING MARKETING TOOLS

Tools make a job easier if you know how to use them appropriately. The following tools will both leverage your time and information and make it easier to operate in your comfort zone.

FIGURE 16–1
Existing Client's Marketing Responsibilities by Level of Responsibility

Engagement Staff Personnel

- Develop sound relationships at assigned levels within the client organization.
- Identify needs for additional services during the engagement, and submit client satisfaction action recommendation to the next level of responsibility.
- Identify up-and-comers in client organization and make their identity known to the appropriate level of responsibility.
- Contribute to the development of client service plans and client business plans as appropriate.

Engagement Management Personnel

- Develop sound relationships at assigned levels within the client organization.
- Develop relationships with up-and-comers.
- Presell needs for additional services.
- Manage the development of client service plans and client business plans.
- Contribute to the development of client referrals by making results visible.

Vice Presidents

- Capitalize on needs identified by staff and presold by engagement manager.
- Assign responsibility for development of client service plans and client business plans and participate in development as appropriate.
- Develop client referrals from satisfied clients.
- Widen and deepen relationships with desirable client executives.
- Undertake upgrading activities with designated clients.
- Determine sources of desirable new clients and capitalize on opportunities.
- Determine reasons for lost clients and take corrective action.

Client service plans. A client service plan is a proprietary document that contains information about the needs, problems, and lost opportunities for a given client. A typical table of contents includes: client background information, such as name and address; financial history with your firm; key client decision makers and quality of relationship with each; description of the client's operation, systems, and major processes; client goals; current problems and opportunities; and your plans for providing additional services.

Project descriptions. A project description covers the need and the events that triggered the project, your approach to solving the need, a copy of the work plan and budget, and a copy of the deliverable. These descriptions are invaluable in planning the next engagement and in describing your experience.

Testimonials from satisfied clients. Letters from satisfied clients are pure gold for use during your prospecting activities.

Problem-approach-results reports (PARs). PARs are one-page mini-descriptions of successful projects. Because they are succinct, they can be read by prospects during a new-business meeting and often swing the prospect over to your way of meeting the need.

Letters of agreement. These letters are summaries of what you agree to do and provide for the client, and also spell out the client's responsibilities. The start and completion dates are mentioned, as well as the method of invoicing.

Client alert reports (CARs). Many of our clients have engaged us to install the CAR system in their business. The CAR is a one-page document that is mandated for use by everyone on the engagement. The CAR briefly describes a need situation uncovered during the current engagement that must be tracked by the engagement supervisor. One of our clients reported an increase of 37 percent in profitable new business using this approach.

To keep the ball rolling, let's turn now to Chapter 17, which focuses on building a responsive marketing organization.

Building a Responsive Marketing Organization

An organization is the systematic arrangement of people, resources, and activities to achieve the objectives set by management. A value-driven organization is responsive to human needs and expectations, builds a culture of empowerment that leads to client satisfaction, and strives for continuous improvement and breakthroughs to reach new heights of client satisfaction. By building an insider's understanding of the niche (the subject of Chapters 13 and 14), you helped ensure that you would be *more* responsive, sensitive, and adaptive to client needs.

Now, you need to organize to ensure that you'll be *highly* responsive to client needs. Stated simply, your goals are to:

1. Be highly responsive to client needs and use your knowledge to deliver value on time, every time, and within budget.

2. Provide consistent, client-centered service that leads to long-term retention of desirable clients.

3. Build value-based relationships with key players in the client organizations and your target markets.

4. Make superior performance leading to client satisfaction the driving force in your firm.

5. Build flexibility and cost containment into all of your systems and processes.

6. Be perceived as one with whom it is easy to do business.

In this chapter, you'll:

☐ Learn the requirements for developing a responsive, performance-driven organization.

☐ Determine ways to build a diamond organization structure for your firm.

☐ Organize your personnel resources to deliver satisfaction while expanding opportunities to provide additional services.

☐ Organize systems, deliverables, and processes for client satisfaction.

DEVELOPING A RESPONSIVE ORGANIZATION

What are the requirements for your firm to become a responsive, performance-driven organization? The chief prerequisites include:

1. Vision: Management spelling out what it sees the organization standing for and becoming, such as "to be the pre-eminent client-centered consulting engineering firm in our market."

2. Major themes derived from management's vision statement, such as "to compete in areas where we have a strategic advantage" or "to have all our staff on alert to leverage everything we do."

3. Challenging plans for building awareness, achieving client satisfaction, and attracting new clients.

4. Building a niche-specific marketing information system.

5. Automating and standardizing repetitive operations and experiences in working with the niche.

6. Establishing value-adding internal training and development designed to raise skill levels of all staff involved in client service and satisfaction.

BUILDING A DIAMOND ORGANIZATION

A new form of organization gaining popularity is called a diamond organization. It's lean on the top and bottom. We recommend that you begin to think in terms of restructuring along the lines of a diamond-shaped organization. There are three levels within a diamond organization: strategic, operational, and administrative.

Strategic Level

Here, top management sets the mission, vision, goals, and values, and participates as appropriate in the marketing activities. Figure 17–1 describes top management's three broad areas of responsibility.

This figure is a useful tool to be used in setting objectives. Several of our clients have a larger version of this chart in their conference

FIGURE 17–1
Top Management's Three Broad Areas of Responsibility

1. *Making your present business effective*
   - Auditing your present practice.
   - Classifying clients by potential and industry–market niche.
   - Identifying prospects and suspects within the niche.
   - Identifying niche influentials.
   - Sloughing off today as needed.
   - Establishing marketing and client service responsibilities.
   - Building your niche's marketing information system.

2. *Identifying and capitalizing on opportunities*
   - Selecting and penetrating target industry–market niches.
   - Developing an insider's understanding and reputation.
   - Building and installing an acquisition process.
   - Expanding services to your existing clients.
   - Acquiring new clients.
   - Converting targets of influence into new leverage relationships.
   - Acquiring niche capacity.

3. *Reinventing your business for your desired future*
   - Reinventing your mission.
   - Sloughing off today as needed.
   - Building strategic alliance partners.
   - Creating a long-term transformation plan.

rooms. They refer to it during staff meetings to continually answer the question, "What marketing and client satisfaction tasks should/could we do now?"

Operational Level

Operations is staffed by full-time personnel and augmented with strategic alliance partners, as well as other contingent workers. Engagement managers oversee strategic alliance partners and contingent workers to provide the power to complete value-adding solutions and powerful deliverables to the client. The virtual organization notion is at play here, meaning that all of the players and all of the resources are identified and charted, but few people actually populate your headquarters or operations center.

Many successful service firms worldwide, even some household names, are operating today with only a few people employed at their headquarters. All the rest are employed via the Internet and managed on-line using Lotus Notes or intranet methods. With this arrangement, you get to keep costs at a minimum and stay more focused on marshaling resources for when and where they are needed.

Administrative Level

Administration is the third component of the diamond organization and is characterized by a lean organization that leverages technology via codified systems and processes. Successful firms find it especially important to develop effective procedures for billing, collecting receivables, and tracking client churn.

ORGANIZING STAFF TO DELIVER SATISFACTION

Let's focus more closely on a crucial aspect of operations, namely, organizing your staff to ensure that clients are satisfied. There are four activities that will enable you to accomplish this:

1. *Appoint a niche point person.* The designated individual must have the responsibility, authority, incentives, and budget to nurture the niche. You want to appoint an experienced, motivated entrepreneurial type of individual. The person's key responsibilities will include tracking changes in the niche, tailoring solutions and support

services to meet emerging needs, coordinating activities, and obtaining and/or providing marketing training so that existing engagements are used effectively to ensure client satisfaction and identify needs for additional services.

2. *Appoint an external niche advisory board.* Such a board, comprised solely of people who are external to your organization, should be staffed with your best clients and niche influentials to ensure that you have a well-rounded board and that their input is timely and vital. Jeff has used such a board for years and credits the success of his Breathing Space® Institute to the advice and feedback of his board.

3. *Appoint an internal niche development committee.* Drawing upon those within your firm, you want to select people from departments and functions who directly provide services to your clients or directly assist the engagement teams.

4. *Tie promotion and career development to meeting responsibilities.* Last but not least, to ensure that client-centered marketing is an active, vibrant part of your firm's raison d'être, you need to assess your staff based on how well they contribute to the firm's overall marketing efforts. When staff members are faced with the choice of either engaging in client-centered marketing or being passed over for promotion, most make the right choice.

ORGANIZING SYSTEMS FOR CLIENT SATISFACTION

How do you know when your firm is a lean, mean client-centered marketing machine? The best clue is when you've successfully automated processes to produce highly leveraged operations. As one successful service marketer commented, "When I can get our repetitive functions down to a 'mindless' state where our staff doesn't have to rethink each action, that's when we get real productivity. The key is thinking it through thoroughly the first time!"

This chapter introduced several key ideas about building an organization to support your marketing initiatives. We move now to a discussion of building the niche's marketing information system (MIS).

CHAPTER 18

Building Your Marketing Information System

You "get smart" about the niche in order to both become and act smart. Obviously this takes niche-specific information and knowledge. Organizing and leveraging the results of your insider's understanding is as important as gaining an insider's understanding in the first place.

Organizing your information requires building and managing a marketing information system. A system is a mechanism with related parts that work together for a purpose and which has greater significance when treated as a whole. You want to build an MIS that codifies and organizes information and knowledge you have on hand so that you are better able to sense, serve, and satisfy the needs of your clients.

After reading this chapter and absorbing the ideas you will be able to:

☐ Understand the purposes of building your MIS.

☐ Define the components of an effective, client-centered MIS.

☐ Determine the databases you need to develop.

PURPOSES OF THE MIS

There are some primary reasons for you to develop a marketing information system:

1. *To leverage your insider's understanding.* Developing an MIS enables you to gain a competitive advantage for having taken the time to learn about a niche.

2. *To build your knowledge base for adding value to your clients.* You will become more valuable to them because of your knowledge and ability to draw upon what you know to devise creative solutions to their need situations.

3. *To support the mission and goals of your business.*

In building your MIS, you make marketing a process. This systematization of client information takes the mystery and much of the misery out of marketing. No longer is it a chance meeting of needs and services. Program development becomes a directed effort. Also, when you to enter data once, you leverage the information time after time.

COMPONENTS OF THE MIS

Building your MIS involves asking the fundamental question, "What information—when and in what form—do I need to sense, serve, and satisfy the needs of clients and others in this niche?" Properly built and managed, your MIS becomes a strategic asset that provides you with a competitive edge that is difficult for competitors to match.

What actually comprises an MIS?

1. The databases where you store files of data for use in all aspects of marketing, selling, and client service.

2. An in-house library where you assemble the key documents used in developing your insider's understanding and in designing tailored solutions.

3. Subject matter files (such as articles about hot-button issues) that are essential for your marketing and client service activities.

Let's tackle these components one at a time.

Building the Niche's Databases

A database is a special compilation of data about a specific marketing topic. Actually, there are at least seven databases you can prepare for a niche:

Clients. Your client database can be your private marketplace where you launch individualized campaigns for a market of one. (With all that you're learning, you will be able to approach clients as individuals.)

Prospects. Your prospects database enables you to turn passive non-clients into active clients by leveraging the information about their buying needs, processes, and preferences.

Suspects. Suspects are nonclient individuals and organizations in your market whom you haven't met. Your suspect database is a pool in which you fish for qualified prospects whom you seek to turn into clients.

Leverage relationships. These are client referrals, nonclient referrals, and niche influentials, the opinion leaders and trendsetters who serve, influence, and regulate the niche players.

Strategic alliance partners. Those who serve the niche in collaborative ways with you represent a valuable resource. This database contains the essential contact information you need to assess the quality and usefulness of the relationships.

Organizations/associations serving and regulating the niche. The organizations serving the niche are worth knowing, and their operations and influence are worth understanding.

Publications. Publications serving the niche need to be identified. You want to build relationships with key editors in working toward becoming known as an insider.

In contemplating how you will collect and maintain the information discussed above, a six-part strategy emerges:

1. *Determine the data you need to collect and enter.* Carefully think through the data fields you will need to make the best use of the database.

2. *Build data entry forms to enter the data.* Several data entry forms were presented in Chapter 3. Use these as thought starters for this task.

3. *Enter the data already on hand.* Much of the data you need in your client-centered database will already be on hand. Locate and enter this data first.

4. *Identify additional data needed.* Blank spaces on the data entry form will identify data that is not already on hand.

5. *Acquire the additional data.* Determine how the data for the missing items on the form can be acquired.

6. *Maintain and update the database.* Establish a system to assure that the data in the databases is kept up to date.

Time marches on; industries change methods of doing business, and contacts change jobs and phone numbers. In a period of a few months to a year, nearly all of your hard work in assembling this data in the first place will be wasted if the data is not updated.

Organizing Your Library

Much of the data gathering you'll undertake to develop your computerized database supports the development of your library. Here are some of the basic items to gather:

1. *The "bibles" used in the niche.* Every industry or profession has certain key manuals or handbooks that are used by the members in their daily operations. These insider books contain vital information about the industry. The next time you are at a client's office, find out what the key reference handbooks are.

2. *Major publications read by clients and prospects.*

3. *Engagement-related materials.* Assemble materials that you will use and refer to frequently, such as:

   Proposals, engagement letters—Analyze these to see which parts are reusable.

   Final reports—Use these as showcase items in new business discussions as evidence of accomplishment.

   Work programs, budgets—Use these in estimating the fees involved in proposed solutions to needs of new clients.

4. *Competitor information.* This includes brochures, statements of capability, copies of proposals, news clippings, press releases, and Web site URLs (uniform resource locators).

5. *Niche data.* Among a variety of items in this category are notes on recent or enduring legislation, trends, and economic studies.

6. *Testimonials from satisfied clients.* These one-page treasures are worth their weight in gold.

Organizing Subject Files

The third major element of your marketing information system (after the databases where you store files of data for use in all aspects of marketing, selling, and client service, and your in-house library where you assemble the key documents used in developing your insider's understanding and in designing tailored solutions) are your subject files.

It is best to organize your subject files around key and emerging topics. Based on your understanding of the niche, on what topics do you need to assemble more in-depth information? Management trends? Administration? New processes? New projects? Yes, in each of these areas.

MAINTAINING AND UPDATING THE MIS

Once your MIS is established, maintain it! Information in the MIS will become outdated quickly if not updated on a periodic basis. It is absolutely critical that you handle this nuts-and-bolts task. You must keep your database, library, and subject files in superb condition. They are as much a part of your overall marketing efforts as the clothes you wear and your in-person presentations. What's more, embarrassing situations could arise if you call on a prospect only to find out that your information is six months out of date because someone didn't update the file.

Hence, updating procedures need to be a part of the daily work routine in your firm. One way to assure updates is to designate an individual to update a client's file whenever a project is initiated, closed, or at another standard milestone. Also, have your staff meet periodically as a group over lunch and update the lists.

You've completed development and refinement of your insider's understanding, built client-centered marketing into the structure of your firm, and even organized to support your new marketing initiatives. Now you are in position to develop value-adding solutions.

CHAPTER 19

Preparing Value-Adding Solutions

In previous chapters, you looked at what's required to build value-adding solutions for clients and you examined factors related to clients' current and potential needs. In this chapter you will learn how to:

☐ Create a name for the solution that "grabs" the communications target.

☐ Prepare a need scenario work sheet.

☐ Outline solution components.

NAME THAT SOLUTION

Your goal is to create a name for the key solution you provide that both positions the solution in the market and defines the core value benefits delivered (costs reduced, productivity increased, sales enhanced, etc.). For example, Dick named his high-intensity one-day seminar "Getting New Clients without Sacrificing Your Professionalism." Selecting this name involved asking and answering:

"Why do our clients need new clients?"

"What objectives are our clients seeking to accomplish?"

"What implications does adding new clients have for their businesses?"

Through trial and error, the title "Getting New Clients without Sacrificing Your Professionalism" emerged. The core value is additional income from new clients. The unique position of the solution in the market (i.e., what competitors are not offering) is getting new clients *without sacrificing your professionalism*. This idea is attractive to service firms, as many professionals tend to resist attending marketing seminars because they feature "selling" techniques.

Jeff named his innovative, one-day seminar "Relaxing at High Speed®." The core value is "relaxing"—not sloughing off, but staying comfortable on the job—something that is of vital concern to career professionals in all industries today, as they are besieged by too much competing for their time and attention. The unique position of the solution in the market is relaxing at *high speed*. This is attractive to career professionals who believe deep down that there must be someone with fresh perspectives and new approaches to remaining productive and competitive, yet balanced and happy. Hence, they are receptive to Jeff's innovative—and proven—methods for getting more done each day and being able to still feel good at the end of the day.

Suppose you offer excellent solutions, but are clueless when it comes to naming them. You could jot down the names of new services and products advertised in the publications serving the niche. Be alert to the opportunities for rearranging and reshuffling various service/product names that you see. Add some of your own terminology to create a unique, fitting name for your solution.

PREPARING A NEED SCENARIO WORK SHEET

The second activity in preparing value-adding solutions involves preparing a need scenario work sheet. When completed, Figure 19–1 will provide you with information to be used in your prospecting, personal selling, and satisfaction activities.

OUTLINING THE SOLUTION COMPONENTS

The third activity in preparing value-adding solutions involves outlining the solution components. There are four major components in

FIGURE 19–1
Need Scenario Work Sheet

The Need
State the need as simply and powerfully as you can using the suspect's or prospect's vocabulary, if appropriate.

The Players

1. *Direct responsibility.* Who in the targeted suspect or prospect organizations is directly responsible for the need you are able to fill? This is where your insider understanding pays dividends.

2. *Others involved.* Who else in the suspect or prospect organization is involved/concerned, and in what ways? Who wants my need solution to succeed (and why)? Who wants my need solution to fail (and why)? Who is going to be affected by the solution and in what ways?

The Consequences

1. *Negative consequences.* What costs and risks are associated with the unmet need? What additional costs and negative consequences are likely to be incurred if the need is not met at this time? What conclusions can you draw as to the nature of the negative consequences, such as: not serious, acceptable risk, serious, critical, unacceptable risk, and so on.

2. *Positive consequences.* What benefits are likely to accrue if the need solution is installed at this time? What new revenue will be generated? What existing revenue will be protected? What costs will be reduced or eliminated? What efficiencies will be introduced? What performance will be improved? What morale will be improved?

The Goal
What is the goal for this need situation? If you've done a good job of defining the need, the goal will often be a restatement of the need statement. Frequently, the goal statement changes a bit due to the in-depth analytical work involved in completing the scenario.

every solution: *favorable conditions, unfavorable conditions, benefits,* and *deliverables.* Let's take each in turn:

Favorable conditions are what already is or will be in place and/or experienced by the client in addition to the deliverables you'll be providing. To identify the favorable conditions ask:

1. What existing favorable conditions will be protected or retained as a result of the solution?

2. What existing favorable conditions will be enhanced?

3. What existing favorable conditions will be added or created?

Unfavorable conditions are negative conditions you're probably going to have to handle, whether the client knows of these or not. To identify such conditions ask:

1. What existing unfavorable conditions need to be eliminated?

2. What existing unfavorable conditions can be minimized?

FIGURE 19–2
Mapping Out a Value-Added Solution: Dick's Program

Proposed solution: full-day seminar on *Getting New Clients without Sacrificing Your Professionalism*

The favorable conditions that will exist upon completion of the training program:

1. The current systems that generate new clients, the existing clients, and documentation that has proven to be successful *will be protected*.

2. The morale of the people involved in prospecting and management's confidence in new client operations *will be enhanced*.

3. New skills *will be added* and information sharpened.

4. Bringing qualified new clients into the practice *will be enhanced*.

The unfavorable conditions that will improve upon completion of the training program:

1. Thoughts and feelings that getting new clients is a talent reserved only for the few natural-born marketers *will be eliminated*.

2. Ineffective actions and procrastination *will be minimized*.

The core benefits from the program:

1. A higher conversion of prospects into clients *will be achieved*.

2. Costs and time involved in unproductive activities *will be reduced*.

The deliverables:

1. The training program structure.

2. The participant materials.

3. What potentially negative conditions can be avoided?

Benefits are the advantages the client will obtain as a result of the solution that you provide. Refer to list of benefits contained in Figure 7–1 presented in Chapter 7.

Deliverables are the tangible products associated with the solution you offer as a result of the engagement. Deliverables could be the progress reports and final report to be presented to the client and the engagement product—a manual, a software program, an organization chart, and the like.

FIGURE 19–3
Mapping Out a Value-Added Solution: Jeff's Program

Proposed solution: full-day seminar on *Relaxing at High Speed*

The favorable conditions that will exist upon completion of the training program:

1. New highly effective ways of approaching the workday ***will be introduced and indoctrinated***.
2. The morale of the people involved in prospecting and management's confidence in new client operations ***will be enhanced***.
3. New ways of collecting, managing, and discarding information ***will be added***.

The unfavorable conditions that will improve upon completion of the training program:

1. Thoughts and feelings that it's impossible to stay on top of important issues ***will subside***.
2. Ineffective activity, procrastination, and time wasting ***will be minimized***.

The core benefits from the program:

1. A greater number of staff members who feel confident in their ability to handle their workload ***will be achieved***.
2. Time involved in and despair over unproductive activities ***will be reduced***.

The deliverables:

1. The training program structure.
2. Participant workbooks, cassettes, and reminder cards.

Your goal is to sketch out or describe the likely form and structure of the deliverables you'll be providing so that you can estimate the level of work you'll need to undertake to both design and deliver the solution.

So, suppose we were to map out for a prospect what could be expected as a result of attending Dick's program on "Getting New Clients without Sacrificing Your Professionalism." See Figure 19–2 for the complete, concise answer.

What could a client expect as a result of scheduling Jeff's program on "Relaxing at High Speed"? See Figure 19–3.

Congratulations! What you have just reviewed is a system for outlining value-adding solutions that can serve you for the rest of your marketing career.

The next chapters will move into the marketing processes comprising the client-centered marketing system.

PART SIX

Developing and Codifying Your Marketing Processes

CHAPTER 20

Positioning Your Business

Positioning is an organized process for finding a entrance point in the minds of your clients and other targets. It is a way of thinking about your market and what's important to the people in it. In developing a position, you educate people about your firm and its value-creating capabilities, and you also differentiate your business from any competition that you know or suspect exists in your target market. Figure 20–1 presents some of the many goals you accomplish when you effectively position your firm.

In completing this chapter, you will:

☐ Be exposed to the six fundamental positioning activities.

☐ Understand what prospects want answered about your firm before hiring you.

☐ Learn about positioning your business against the competition.

☐ Know how to position your firm with the various players in the niche.

POSITIONING ACTIVITIES

There are six fundamental positioning activities that in combination help to achieve a strong position in your market niche. The six activities are:

FIGURE 20–1
Positioning Accomplishes at Least Four Goals

1. Being seen as "somebody special to some special bodies."
2. Leveraging your insider's understanding.
3. Contributing to and supporting your awareness process activities.
4. Establishing credibility with key players in the niche.

1. Positioning your business with targets of opportunity.

2. Positioning your business against the competition.

3. Positioning your people with targets of opportunity.

4. Positioning your strategic alliance partners with targets of opportunity.

5. Positioning your solutions with targets of opportunity.

6. Positioning your solutions against the competition.

Positioning Your Business with Targets of Opportunity

Targets who don't know you personally have at least three questions they need answered before they consider meeting with you to discuss using your firm:

Q1. Who are these people?

Q2. What do they do, and for whom?

Q3. What value can they bring to my operation?

You can help to answer these questions for them by first determining the answers to your own satisfaction. (See Figure 20–2.)

Positioning Your Business against the Competition

Suppose we asked you, "How are you different from (known) competitors?" and "How are you better than (known) competitors?" To answer the first question, list the factors that make your business different from competitors. Factors could include:

FIGURE 20–2
Three Things Targets Want to Know about You

Q1. Who are these people? Begin by determining the nature of your business.

"We are a _____ firm."

What type of firm are you?

Professional service.
Business service.
Consulting.
Marketing consulting.
Other.

Q2. What do they do and for whom? State clearly your mission/purpose for being in business.

"We do _____ (what) for _____ (whom)."

Answering the "what we do" portion requires some thoughtful analysis. Rather than listing a number of services provided, the client-centered marketer specifies the value-adding factors brought to clients. A good way to begin is to revisit the core benefits of:

Improving something of value to the clients.
Reducing the cost of something.
Adding something of value.
Protecting something of value.
Eliminating some unwanted condition.

Answering the "for whom" is simple—for clients and prospects in your niche's market.

Q3. What value can they bring to my operation? State your promise made to your market. This promise may take one of two forms: a slogan or a statement. For example:

"Federal Express gets your packages there absolutely positively overnight."

"We are a full-service computer consulting firm. If it works on a PC, we have the people and know-how to handle your needs. Our services and training aid you in using the computer without having to become a technical wizard."

In this step, you are developing what is often called your "elevator patter," the simple, powerful, and cogent description of your firm and its core value-adding activity.

- Your time in the market.

- Niche-specific experience.

- The number of prestige clients served.

- Your core business philosophy.

- Relationships with niche influentials.

- Your community involvement.

To this list, add any factors that are unique to your business. Even though at first you may "run out of gas," dig deep to find these points. When you have compiled a somewhat lengthy list, ask the question of your best clients and others in the niche who know you. Their answers will often give you valuable insights and more points to add to your list.

From this master list, select a few factors that are truly different from other firms, are known to be important to the clients you seek and serve, and for which you readily have evidence, particularly for communication with your prospects.

The second question on the minds of your targets as you attempt to position your business against the competition is, "How are you better?" Consultant Marcus Bogue opines, "[I]t doesn't matter how good you are; it only matters how relatively good you are. If someone else is better than you are, it doesn't matter how good *you* are." If you agree with Bogue, then answering this question means that you need to focus on the ways you add value to your clients that are better than the competition.

The competitive advantages you can create for your clients might consist of any of the following:

- You provide training that gets the solution installed faster and more completely.

- You help the client to leverage resources in ways the client never realized.

- You have codified and made available to your clients insights and lessons learned that you distilled from your years of practice.

Positioning Your People with Targets of Opportunity

Positioning, in this respect, means that you showcase your people by communicating:

1. Who they are: their names, ages, education, training, and so forth.

2. What they do for clients: the solutions they are capable of providing.

3. Why they are truly valuable to the targets: the special value they bring to the client, such as niche-specific experience, special training, affiliations, and certifications.

For each of your staff who have contact with your clients, you should develop a client-centered bio-sketch or client-centered resume that covers these three factors. This bio-sketch can be used each time you discuss your staff with prospects and clients in this niche.

Be sure not to use the typical resume often prepared for seeking employment. Job-seeking resumes tend to list too many things in a too-passive format.

Positioning Your Strategic Alliance Partners with Targets of Opportunity

In today's rapidly changing business environment, the number and quality of your strategic alliance partners is often the tiebreaker when competing for new business. Remember, strategic alliance partners are the cooperative relationships you have with others who serve the market and add complementary skills and resources to your solution capability. Your method in positioning strategic alliance partners is the same as with your people; you need to prepare a bio-sketch that clearly outlines the three showcasing factors mentioned.

Positioning Your Solutions with Targets of Opportunity

Here is where your insider's understanding is extremely valuable. You want to look for the key buying factors your clients consider, such as: competitive fees, niche experience, quick response time, and innovative solutions.

Your task is to select the client's actual key buying factors and clearly state how your solution fully meets each factor. For example, when discussing quick response time you could say, "Our goal is to return phone calls or faxed messages within four hours and sooner if there is an emergency. Our clients have three ways to contact us: by phone, by beeper, and by E-mail."

Positioning Your Solutions against the Competition

Prospects who don't know you personally will have at least two questions in this area about you and what you offer:

1. How is your solution different from (known) competitors' solutions?
2. How is your solution better than (known) competitors' solutions?

In answering the first question, ask yourself "What is it about my solution that makes it different from the competition?" Consider:

- The scope of the solution.
- The technology used.
- Your people and strategic alliance partners.
- The deliverable(s) you produce with the solution.

Add to this list any other factors that make your solution different. As before, dig deep to find these points, and, when you have a workable list, ask the question of your best clients and others who know you in the niche.

From the completed list of factors that make your solution different from the competitors', select a few points that are distinctly different, important to the clients you seek and serve, and for which you have readily available evidence for communication with your prospects.

In answering the "How is your solution better?" question, consider your competitive advantages. A competitive advantage is a strength, image, person, or process that is valued by clients and prospects in your niche. It is something perceived by the client as being only or more readily available from you than from others offering your type of solution. Consider the following possible competitive advantage factors:

- Your niche experience.
- Your people.
- Your codified engagement process steps.
- Your automated engagement process steps.
- Your deliverable installation process.

Add to this list other competitive advantages you have and can in-stall in your client's operations. As before, dig deep and ask around, so that you end up with a strong list.

You have now completed a lengthy but worthwhile process that will enable you to communicate about your firm, its people, and its solu-tions with your clients and prospects in ways that are valuable to the clients and that give you leverage over the competition.

CHAPTER 21

Building Your Firm's Intended Image

An image is a mental picture of something not present. In a business context, one dictionary defines image as "a general or public perception, as of a company, especially when achieved by calculation aimed at creating goodwill." Some think of a firm's image as its external "personality."

After completing this chapter you will:

☐ Learn the difference between intended image and actual image.

☐ Know the steps in building the image you desire.

☐ Be able to identify possible value drivers important to clients.

☐ Draw upon a mix of image-building activities.

It's been said that everything about an organization talks. Indeed, clients form impressions of your business from you and your staff, your facilities, stationery, and a host of other cues. In terms of client-centered marketing, the term *intended image* refers to the picture of your firm as an external, specialized insider resource that you seek to communicate through your client service and awareness activities.

The actual image of your firm is the sum total of perceptions by clients and others of your company; thus, your firm's image is "owned" by those over whom you have little direct control.

The image of your business that others maintain is comprised of the set of beliefs, ideas, and impressions that they hold about your firm whether they have direct, firsthand experience with you or not. If there is no direct contact with a representative of your firm, then their perception of your firm is based on a general image they've conceived from word-of-mouth publicity, experience in dealing with your type of firm, and, perhaps, encountering your promotional activities.

STEPS IN BUILDING THE FIRM'S INTENDED IMAGE

You consciously design and attempt to build your firm's intended image to support and maximize both the impact of your positioning strategy and the effect of your promotional activities on your targets of opportunity, attention, and influence.

Step 1

Start by asking and answering this question: "How must we be seen, and by whom, to support our positioning strategy and be successful against our competition?" A key aspect of your desired image might be to have clients and influentials think and say of you, "These people are good; they know our business and our challenges; they've been around for awhile, and are strong enough to stay around during challenging times."

How, precisely, do you want to be seen? As expensive and worth it? Or as good value for a low price? Do you want to be seen as any of the following?

- Someone with whom it's easy to do business.
- Innovator.
- Coach.
- Educator.
- Trailblazer.

Craig Gibson, vice president of marketing for Cambridge Transnational Associates, a Boston-based firm, seeks to have his organization regarded as responsive, accessible, and credible, particularly by companies in the Northeastern United States who are considering launching an international business initiative.

Building your insider's understanding (the theme of Chapters 13 and 14) enabled you to identify the possible value drivers important to clients in the niche. Figure 21–1 can help you select the elements/components of your intended image.

Step 2

Ask and answer this question: "How are we probably seen by those we identified in step one?" This is no time for desk-driven research. You need to meet with your clients and listen to what they may tell you about your image. Talk also with others who serve the niche to get insights into your probable image.

Step 3

Complete the analysis by asking and answering this question: "What needs to be done to achieve our intended image?" Steps 1 and 2 were gap analysis. This step is gap closing and requires relatively simple, timely, and inexpensive image-building activities that will leverage the resources available to you.

DEVELOPING YOUR MIX OF IMAGE-BUILDING ACTIVITIES

Your goal is to develop a mix of image-building activities that are within your comfort zone, are consistent with the expectations of the niche players, and are within the resource capabilities of your business. The following are some promotional activities that meet the criteria:

Capitalize on publicity opportunities. To further enhance your firm's image, you need to identify and capitalize on available publicity opportunities, such as writing letters to the editor, opinion pieces, and educational flyers.

Speak to local groups. Speaking to the right groups builds credibility and a favorable awareness among targeted niche players. Your goal is to identify and speak before promotional forums, a marketing term for large groups of useful and potentially useful niche players. Chapter 22 covers this in depth.

Write for publications read by your clients and targets. Writing offers a number of benefits: You can address large audiences, thereby leveraging your time and other resources; you can enhance your reputation; and you

FIGURE 21–1
Determining Value Drivers to Highlight

RELIABILITY involves consistency of performance and dependability. It means that your firm performs the service right the first time and that you honor your promises. Specifically, it involves accuracy in billing, keeping records correctly, and performing the service at the designated time.

RESPONSIVENESS concerns the willingness and readiness of you and your staff to provide service. Specifically, it involves, for example, sending a transaction slip immediately, calling a client or prospect back quickly, and giving prompt service (e.g., setting up appointments as requested).

COMPETENCE means possessing the required skills and knowledge to perform the services you purport to offer. It involves knowledge and skill of the contact personnel and of the operational support personnel.

ACCESS involves being approachable and easy to reach (i.e., your telephone lines are not incessantly busy and callers are not put on hold), minimal waiting time to receive service (e.g., at a bank), convenient hours of operation, and convenient locations.

COURTESY involves politeness, respect, consideration, and friendliness of contact personnel (including receptionists, telephone operators, etc.). It also includes consideration for the client's property (e.g., no muddy shoes on the carpet) and clean and neat appearance of public contact personnel.

COMMUNICATION means listening to clients and prospects and keeping them informed in language they can understand. It may require that you adjust your language for different clients, increasing the level of sophistication with a well-educated client, and speaking simply and plainly with a novice. It also involves explaining your services, their costs, and trade-offs between service and cost. In addition, it means assuring the clients that a problem will be handled.

CREDIBILITY means conveying trustworthiness, believability, and honesty. It involves having the client or prospect's best interests at heart. Many factors contribute to credibility, such as your company name and reputation, the personal characteristics of your contact people, and the degree (or avoidance) of hard sell involved in interactions with the client or prospect.

(Continued)

FIGURE 21–1   Continued

SECURITY is enabling your clients to have freedom from danger, risk, or doubt in using your services.

KNOWING AND UNDERSTANDING THE CLIENT/PROSPECT involves making the effort to understand clients' or prospects' specific needs. It means learning their specific requirements, providing individualized attention, and offering them recognition.

TANGIBLES include the physical evidence of the service you provide, such as the project deliverables, the appearance of your staff personnel, the condition of the tools or equipment you use, even the condition and appearance of your office.

---

can build favorable awareness of your experience and capabilities. Chapters 23 and 24 discuss the procedures involved.

Showcase your people. Design the personal image you want your staff people to convey. For example, what is the appropriate wardrobe for you and your people? In which community activities will you participate? What are the memberships that you will seek?

As discussed in Chapter 20, you'll want to prepare result-oriented bio-sketches of your key people, including their niche-specific experience, key credentials, and certifications such as CPA, PE, or CMC, and identify your staff's and firm's affiliations and the benefits these affiliations deliver to your clients. In showcasing your people, we also suggest assigning a niche point person to represent the niche and build relationships with the media.

Design the atmospherics of your business. Ensure that your office setup is consistent with the image you wish to convey. Among many factors to consider are these:

- Telephone receptionist: human voice or digital.
- Location and type of structure.
- Entrance, waiting area, and publications available.
- Your office, awards, and plaques.
- Library and operations area.

Your corporate identity is the clothing covering your firm's personality and is influenced by your logo, graphics, and letterhead; the color and feel of paper you use; and the family of publications you've produced, such as brochures, capability statements, and annual reports.

PUTTING IT ALL TOGETHER

Commit your analysis of your firm's image at present to writing. Then, distribute it to your staff and to clients who have your best interests at heart. Determine if the intended image does in fact match up with the image others have of you. Then, take the appropriate steps to close any gaps you encounter.

CHAPTER 22

Speaking to Targeted Groups

Speaking to targeted groups in the niche can be an enjoyable way of creating a favorable awareness of you and your firm. Many opportunities exist for speaking to targeted groups, and you can create additional opportunities.

After completing this chapter you'll know:

- ☐ What is the best way to position yourself to be invited to an organization.

- ☐ What type of letter should be sent describing your topics.

- ☐ What tips should be followed to increase your effectiveness.

- ☐ The key components of delivering a speech from a script.

- ☐ Why you should make sure your presentation is taped.

- ☐ Why you should always provide handouts for the audience.

Many local organizations, such as chambers of commerce and civic and charitable associations, actively seek speakers. Yet, the program chair of these groups often must scramble to find an interesting speaker.

If you give a good presentation as a volunteer speaker to local groups, and are, in fact, able to influence the audience. Rest assured that you'll be contacted by individual members at some point in the future regarding professional services.

POSITIONING TO SPEAK

The best way to position yourself to be invited to speak to a local organization is to be a member of that organization. This strategy ties in with the need to join charitable and civic associations.

The authors have consistently applied this principle and in recent years have spoken to the following groups, of which one or both have been members:

International Platform Association.

Institute of Management Consultants.

Greater Washington Society of Association Executives.

Active Corps of Executives.

American Marketing Association.

National Speakers Association.

International Toastmasters.

SPREADING THE WORD

An excellent way to spread the word that you are available for seminar presentations is to type a one-page letter explaining who you are, giving a little about your background and a one-line or short paragraph description of three to five topics on which you are prepared to speak. This letter could easily be photocopied and distributed by your clerical staff to 50 to 100 groups in the local area. As a result of this mailing and depending on how well known you are in the community, two to five speaking engagements may be generated. A sample letter appears in Figure 22–1.

For this or any other mailing, it is wise to send a second letter or to have someone on your staff make a follow-up phone call to each of the

FIGURE 22–1
Sample Speaker's Letter

Alvin I. Speakeasy
Consultants Unlimited
10 Orator Avenue
Wichita Falls, TX
(817) 444-4444

Dear Meeting Planner:

Your organization may have need for a speaker with my experience and qualifications. I have been a management consultant serving businesses and government agencies since 1982. I have had numerous speaking engagements and written several articles on effectively managing a business.

My most frequently requested topics are:

How to trim expenses when there's nothing left to trim.

How to attract, motivate, and retain young executives.

The record-keeping aspects of managing your business.

Eight ways to save on advertising expense.

Incorporating a firm.

How to find the right consultant for your business.

How to prepare a loan application package.

Your interest is appreciated. Feel free to call me at the number above to discuss any of the topics listed.

Yours truly,

Alvin I. Speakeasy

organizations receiving your letter. This reinforces each recipient's knowledge of your desire to speak.

Even when contacting meeting planners who represent small groups, consider that the people whom you are trying to reach are very busy. Whether they love your topics or are indifferent to them, chances are they may not get back to you in a timely fashion or may not get back to you at all. It is your responsibility to ensure that your initial communications are received and understood. As with personal selling, the incidence of your speaking to a particular group will be highly dependent on the level and adequacy of the interpersonal communication between you and the meeting planner. The more precisely you can describe what you wish to present to the group and the more empathetic you are to the group's needs, the higher the probability that they will invite you to speak.

Accepting and Negotiating

The time, the setting, and the format of the speech are usually set by the host organization. You will usually be requested to speak for 30 or 45 minutes with 10 or 15 minutes for a question-and-answer session. The group's meeting planner or program host can fill you in on details regarding scheduling information.

Ask the meeting planner for a copy of the membership directory and list of attendees. If you're giving a major talk to a major group at a conference, you can send the key attendees a letter introducing yourself and suggest to meet them during the conference.

Planning

We suggest that you invest 40 percent in planning the talk, 30 percent in delivering it, and 30 percent in working the room before and after the talk. Planning involves developing a catchy topic (see the sample letter in Figure 22–1). We usually work without notes or with a brief outline. If notes, outlines, cue cards, and other helpers support your efforts, use them!

Be sure to provide quality handouts printed on your firm's letterhead so that attendees may readily remember you and perhaps call you in the future. (See page 164.)

DELIVERING YOUR TALK LIKE A PRO

Volumes have been written on how to deliver an effective speech. The most effective speakers are those who operate without a net—they don't read from a script or use notes. These are pros who speak for a living, have delivered their speeches over and over, and know exactly when to pause, when to get a laugh, and when to come on strong. Since most professionals don't speak for a living, it is advisable to prepare notes or, if necessary, to work from a script.

We recommend jotting down a few key words on a page rather than producing a full-blown script. Each key word generally is worth two to five minutes of presentation time. To deliver a 30-minute speech, 10 key words on a page, each representing about three minutes of presentation time, ideally, are all the notes that you need.

If you are more comfortable with a script, then, by all means, have it typed in abnormally large print with plenty of spacing so that you can find your place easily when you are standing at the lectern. The chart in Figure 22–2 will carry you through the process of delivering your talk like a pro, particularly if you are using a script.

Making Impact

Plant the seed of need and offer a solution. For example, you might say, "Several of the best ways to handle the issue include. . . ." This encourages the listener to believe that there are still other ways that you know about.

- Conduct mini-polls. When speaking to a captive audience—and that is exactly what your listeners will be—you can poll them on various issues. In addition to bolstering your understanding of the niche, you can develop these mini-polls as news releases. The information and feedback you gain from one presentation can immediately be used in subsequent presentations, rapidly increasing your reputation in the niche.

- Questions from attendees are invaluable. After your speech, have attendees ask you questions on hot-button and recurring-need areas that were not addressed during your presentation. The issues raised during these sessions can serve as automatic guideposts for

FIGURE 22–2
Deliver Your Talk Like a Pro—Working from a Script

A. *Make a readable script.*

1. Make the script readable at a glance. Use double space or even triple space on just one side of the paper.
2. Use a speaking language.
3. Underscore key words.
4. Put a diagonal mark between words where you want to pause.
5. Number your pages.

B. *Settle the butterflies.*

1. Take a few deep breaths while waiting to be introduced.
2. Review your opening lines.

C. *Approach with enthusiasm.*

1. Come on with enthusiasm and smile.
2. If you have a lot of notes and props, have them at the lectern ahead of time.

D. *Open with style.*

1. Take about five seconds to arrange your notes before you start to speak to let yourself and the audience relax.
2. Say "Good morning" or whatever is appropriate.
3. Thank the person who introduced you. Tell why you're glad to be there.
4. Compliment the audience in some manner.

E. *Read the way you would talk.*

1. As you finish a page, slide it across to expose the next one. Look at the audience, pause slightly, and they won't realize you did it.
2. Scan a few lines ahead so you can look at the audience frequently as you speak.
3. Pause now and then as though thinking of the right word even though it's right there in the script.
4. Talk directly to the audience as much as possible and talk to people on the left, in the middle, and on the right.
5. Don't lean on the podium.
6. If you fluff a line, ignore it or laugh it off.

F. *Use humor—but watch out.*

1. One-liners are the safest humor for the nonprofessional.

G. *That parting smile.*

When you come to the close of your talk, put your notes aside, look out at the audience, moving your attention from one group to another while you give your closing statement. Tell them how great they were, and express your wishes for their success. Put your arm up as a farewell greeting and smile as you walk off.

tailoring and enhancing your promotional and services-delivery systems.

- Hold a business card drawing at the conclusion of your presentation. Ask a member of the sponsoring organization to gather business cards from each person for the drawing. The prize we offer is an autographed copy of one of our books. The prize you offer can be any book of quality, whether or not you wrote it. The recipient instantly becomes your friend and booster. This drawing has several benefits. First, it holds the audience's attention and enables you to establish personal contact. Second, you obtain names and identifying data that you might not have gotten just from the attendance list.

HONING YOUR EFFORTS

As you start to get requests to speak, you will need additional information, such as the size and setup of the meeting (see Figure 22–3). A checklist of items you should determine to increase your effectiveness on the day or night of your presentation is given in Figure 22–4.

QUESTIONS FOR REFLECTION

Bruce Harrison, president of the E. Bruce Harrison Company, a public relations firm based in Washington, DC, suggests reflecting on the following 20 questions in your quest to become an effective speaker:

1. How do I get people to listen?
2. When do I start speaking?
3. How do I handle nervousness?
4. What am I doing here?
5. How do I handle questions?
6. How do I handle hostile questions?
7. Should I be aggressive?
8. How do I take charge?
9. How do I not sound defensive?
10. What if I am not an expert?

FIGURE 22–3
Meeting Room Setup

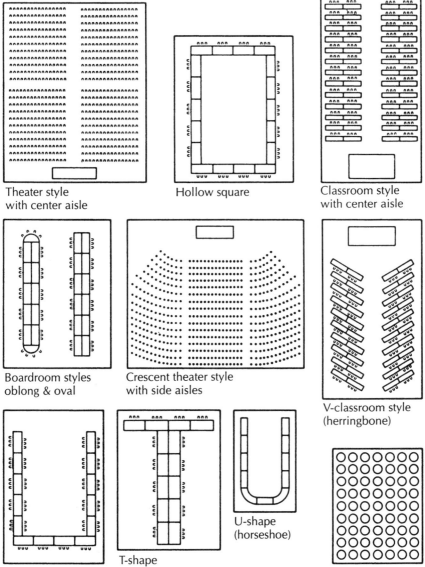

Theater style
with center aisle

Hollow square

Classroom style
with center aisle

Boardroom styles
oblong & oval

Crescent theater style
with side aisles

V-classroom style
(herringbone)

Standard U-shape

T-shape

U-shape
(horseshoe)

Round tables

FIGURE 22–4
Checklist for Effective Speaking Engagement

☐ Size of room.	☐ Audiovisual equipment.
☐ Setup, staging.	☐ Surrounding rooms.
☐ Number of attendees.	☐ Temperature.
☐ Program length.	☐ Lighting.
☐ Sound system.	☐ Audience composition.

11. What if I don't know the answer?

12. What if the question is dumb?

13. Should I smile more?

14. Should I try tc gesture?

15. Where do I look when I speak?

16. Where do I look when I am not speaking?

17. If I can't comment, what can I do?

18. Can I fudge the facts?

19. How can I tell if I am scoring?

20. Where are the restrooms?

OPENING NIGHT

Here are some guidelines for making your presentation:

1. *Posture* should be erect and poised.

2. *Hand gestures* should be made mainly between the shoulder and the waist and be appropriate to the material presented.

3. *Body movements*, if made, should be stable and appropriate to the material.

4. *Vocal production* must be audible and geared to the size of the audience.

5. *Vocal intonation* should be varied.

6. *Vocal rate* should be appropriate to the size of the audience and the material presented.

7. *Articulation* must be clear and precise.

8. *Delivery* should have few or be absent of audible pauses.

9. *Eye movement* should make contact regularly with the audience.

10. *Approaching and leaving* should be deliberate.

GET YOUR SPEECH ON TAPE

Every speaker should insist on being taped while making a presentation to a live audience. Why? There are five reasons:

1. *Taping affords personal review of the presentation.* There is no better way to review your performance than to hear exactly what you said and how you said it, on tape.

2. *Each tape is potentially salable.* Tape cassette producers, manufacturers, and distributors can professionally edit your tape, supplying voiceovers and transition passages that can result in a salable cassette. Keep in mind that there are other audiences similar to the one to whom you spoke. It may pay for you to be able to repeat your presentation on tape.

3. *The tape transcript is salable.* Don't overlook the value of marketing the tape transcript to members of the group you addressed. Professional societies frequently offer tape transcripts from symposia and seminars that they have sponsored to those members who were not able to attend or who wish to have a written record of what was said in the speech.

4. *The transcript can be converted into articles.* Frequently, a transcript of as few as three or four pages lends itself to being turned into an excellent article. Every writer finds it easier to start from an established base and make editorial changes than to face four blank pages and begin writing. With longer transcripts, it may be

possible to extract several excellent articles, which, in turn, can be used to promote your speaking career and earn additional income.

5. *Use tapes to get other speaking engagements.* After your speaking engagement has been taped, you can extract a 5- to 10-minute passage that can be used to develop demonstration tapes for distribution to other meeting planners. What better way for them to assess your speaking skills than to hear a passage from a live performance?

HELPING THE AUDIENCE TO REMEMBER YOU

Many novice speakers make the mistake of cutting and running after their presentation. Stick around for at least 30 minutes, and possibly longer. Take full advantage of the leveraging opportunities that exist when you have a room full of prospective clients and nonclients.

As mentioned, distribution of article reprints or other written material along with the speaking engagement provides the audience with an opportunity to secure the correct name and address of the speaker. Thus, it always makes good sense to give out something with your presentation. On the other hand, don't attempt to make a sales pitch or sales presentation; merely speak on a topic of interest and do your best. Never expect a speech or presentation to bring instant results. Altman and Weil, a professional services consulting firm, reports that it received telephone calls from targets who heard a member of the firm speak several years previously.

One way to ensure participation by the group to whom you speak is to offer a handout that contains some fill-in-the-blank–type exercises. By giving members of your listening audience a task to perform (i.e., to make the handouts that they have received more complete), you raise their interest level and the probability that they will retain your material.

Consultants and professional service providers who frequently speak to groups find that it is a faux pas to circulate all of the handouts at once. With a three-page handout, for example, distribute each page as your presentation progresses. This reduces the incidence of attendees flipping the pages and getting ahead of you. It is a little more effort to circulate the pages individually, but doing so provides a brief vocal pause for you, and a mental pause for your listeners. In advance, you can share with the meeting planner the manner in which you wish to have seminar materials distributed.

Your decision on whether to seek speaking engagements as a personal promotional tool hinges on your ability to be interesting and have something worthwhile to say to a group composed of targets of opportunity or influence. If you've never spoken before a group, you have a unique experience in store. Everyone is nervous at first, but, before long, you may find speaking quite exhilarating.

CHAPTER 23

Writing That Works

Your firm can enjoy a large number of benefits when you have an article printed in a business or professional publication. There are also, however, some misconceptions about what getting published will do for the firm.

Upon completing this chapter, you will have learned:

☐ Some of the primary benefits of getting published.

☐ The best topics for articles.

☐ The basic steps in writing an article, starting from scratch.

☐ How you can easily overcome writer's block.

☐ What place getting an article published has in your overall marketing effort.

☐ How you can get mentioned in the articles others are writing.

PUBLISHING OPPORTUNITIES ABOUND

The number of general, industrial, business, professional, and in-house publications has risen dramatically in the last 10 years. By using *Bacon's Magazine Directory*, the *Magazine Industry Market Place*, *Working Press of the Nation Writer's Market*, *Standard Periodicals Directory*, or *Gebbie's All in One Directory*, you can obtain the name, address, telephone number, editorial content, fees paid, circulation, target audience, and submission requirements for thousands of journals and magazines!

All of the publications you identified in establishing your niche database and library are excellent places to send an article. Given all the information you have assembled about the niche, it would not be difficult to determine several interesting topics. Your article need not be more than 750 to 1000 words (three or four doublespaced typed pages). As long as you simply address one of the hot buttons or recurring needs of readers, the probability of your article being accepted and published will be high.

Articles written by your competition are must reading. Study them to see how you might use *their* articles to help you make your selling point to suspects in *your* niche.

There are also countless newsletters in the United States today and thousands more worldwide, and the number is growing at an exponential rate. The *Newsletter Yearbook Directory* and the *Oxbridge Directory of Newsletters* are particularly useful. Publication in newsletters may yield the same actual benefits as can be achieved through publication in the larger trade magazines.

Take advantage of the pyramid process when trying to get published. It is far easier to get a small column published in a newsletter than in a major, nationwide magazine serving your targeted industry. Once you get published in a newsletter, make an attractive reprint, write the words "previous publication" in the corner and include that reprint when sending out other manuscripts to editors of larger publications.

The net benefits for you and your firm, of course, are contingent on the match between the target market of the newsletter and your targets of opportunity and influence. For a magazine or a journal, ask for a sample issue to review, and later write to the editor to relay your article theme.

BENEFITS OF GETTING PUBLISHED

The primary benefits of getting published include the following:

1. Building the firm's reputation.
2. Creating a favorable impression.

3. Bolstering the firm's marketing tools.

4. Providing or generating inquiries.

5. Being invited to speak to groups.

Let's examine each benefit in detail.

Getting published *helps build your firm's reputation* in the article topic area. If a partner in an engineering firm, for example, writes an article on reinforcing bridge supports, a public notice has been made that the firm has expertise in this area and may provide assistance in this area. A similar example can be drawn for nearly any topic.

You can *create a favorable impression* by supplying associates with a reprint of an article you have published. Modesty aside, most authors are very proud of their work and have no qualms about submitting reprints to friends, relatives, and associates. Most business associates are pleased and impressed to accept your article reprint. Although they may not say so directly, they may also revel in your small glory and serve as ambassadors for you by informing others.

Many firms maintain in reception areas a notebook that includes the articles and publications of their employees. The articles discuss a wide variety of topics within the fields of specialization. Visitors to the office are impressed by the writing skills and subject expertise of the company staff.

Another benefit of getting published is that the publication or article reprint helps *bolster your firm's brochures and marketing portfolios.* You can include reprints in all your correspondence, including proposals. A high-quality article reprint on glossy stock also increases the effect of a direct-mail campaign.

The placement of articles in professional or trade journals may *generate inquiries from potential clients.* After a writer from a local public relations firm has an article published in the Sunday edition of the newspaper (perhaps in the business and finance section or in the style section), some phone calls and inquiries may be generated as a direct result. For magazine publications, readership response to the article is less clearly defined. However, some readers viewing the article may (1) clip or photocopy the article for future reference and (2) contact you for further information, comments, or assistance.

A final benefit is that an article will often result in your *being invited to speak* before a particular group. In actuality, every article can be made into a speech and vice versa. Thus, the opportunity to repeat your message locally to defined markets should not be overlooked.

Although the ability to speak or write is essential, this ability does not necessarily have to be yours. If writing isn't one of your strong points, or you can't afford the time required for preparation, consider hiring assistance. Freelance journalists, college professors, and graduate students are often excellent writers to hire on a part-time basis. You provide the content. They organize and write the speech or article.

SELECTING ARTICLE TOPICS

The best topics for articles are derived from the successful work that you have already done. This may include reports, papers, summaries, guides, exhibits, and so on that you previously presented to a client, which can be generalized and applied to a larger audience. You may wish to write an article *with* a client for whom you have produced exceptional results.

Other good topics for articles include those topics that can be addressed by you or any members of the staff. If you're an architect, you may have an excellent article on "tips for success when designing skywalks" in your mind, even though you may never have written about the topic. Any topic that can readily be addressed by you or your staff and is of interest to your selected market is a good topic.

If you are developing your credentials in a specific market or functional area, then, by all means, a topic in that specified market or area on which you can write intelligently is an excellent choice. An article that stresses benefits to your clients as a result of working with you is particularly useful.

GENERATING ARTICLE TOPICS

Here are some ways to generate article topics and enable you to get started on the high road to getting published:

1. Make a list of gripes or discomforts in connection with your profession. Regardless of where you work or what you do, a list of gripes can readily be created. Within each gripe lies the seed of a subject for an article. If something bothers you, it undoubtedly bothers others in your field. Discuss the problem in broad industry terms and offer suggestions for redress. The authors have done this on several occasions on the topics of management, marketing, and starting new ventures. By recognizing the universality of a problem that you face in your profession, you will instantly be creating material for an excellent article.

2. Start a clip file of articles that interest you. Every time you read the Sunday newspaper or a professional journal, save those articles that strike your fancy. File all the clippings by topic or subject area. Months later, review your clip file, and, to your amazement, you will see that what you've clipped serves as the catalyst for numerous article ideas. Freelance writers have successfully used the clip file technique for years.

3. Develop a list of six or eight ways to do something better. The market for how-to articles is increasing steadily as more and more clients thirst for do-it-yourself information. By introducing a number into the title of the article, such as "Eight Ways to Accomplish XYZ," you have established a hook that will appeal to your selected target market.

4. Recall your favorite professional experience, biggest disappointment, or other memorable event. If you've been practicing for more than a year, undoubtedly you will have a number of interesting experiences, and these make good starting points for articles.

5. Shorten or adapt larger articles, reports, or papers that you've already done. The fastest way to write an article is not to write, but, rather, to glean the essence of previous work, update it, improve it, or prepare it from a different perspective. We've gone back through old consulting reports and quickly found two that could be readily converted to publishable articles.

6. Take a contrary view to a popular opinion or method for accomplishing something. With great care and sound reasoning, gently but convincingly explain why your view or approach is superior or more effective.

Here's a checklist of additional ideas for generating article topics:

☐ Interview a prominent person in your industry.

☐ Make a list of new developments in your profession.

☐ Discuss new legislation, regulations, or other official changes in an industry and how it (they) will impact the reader.

DICTATING: THE END OF WRITER'S BLOCK

An effective way to conquer writer's block is by using the portable dictation equipment that has long been available with countless features at a wide variety of prices. The vast majority of professionals still either write out articles in longhand, type them onto a disk, or dictate them to a secretary who transcribes from shorthand. These three methods are prone to writer's block, and furthermore are grossly inefficient for the purposes of writing articles and optimizing the use of time.

When it comes to typing or writing longhand versus using portable dictation equipment, the difference is like walking or driving a car in order to reach a destination. Once you become familiar with the ease of operation, the convenience, and the pure joy of finishing articles in approximately one-third of the time it used to take you, you'll never again let yourself be without portable dictation equipment. You will probably start taking it with you on trips and after hours to record notes and ideas, to finish letters immediately after meetings, and to get to all the articles that you have wanted to write, but never found the time to do so.

The reason why most professionals haven't converted to portable dictation equipment, based on industry surveys, is that they feel a strong need to see what they are working on. A visual review is indeed helpful; however, this is not a reason to avoid portable dictation equipment. Two factors should be considered:

1. To properly use portable dictation equipment, you must first prepare a good outline of the material to be dictated, just as if you were initiating a handwritten article. With the outline, key words can be expanded to sentences and paragraphs through dictation. The pause feature on all portable dictation equipment allows you to

start and stop at any time to gather thoughts and to articulate complete sentences and paragraphs.

The paragraph just completed required three pauses while dictating; however, as the secretary transcribed the material directly from the tape, there were no unusually long breaks in any sentences (other than those created through use of the foot pedal that controls the speed).

Portable dictation machines have recall and playback features that allow you to monitor your recording as it progresses. With a good outline, however, your need to review what has been dictated diminishes directly proportional with use of the equipment. The start-up time to become familiar and then proficient with the equipment should average no more than an hour.

2. The need for visual review is overestimated. As you are writing longhand or typing onto a disk, there is a strong need for visual review because you are progressing so slowly. When you are dictating, your mind is working much more rapidly than you can write or even type. As you dictate passages and paragraphs in 30 or 40 seconds that formerly required much more time, the need for visual review diminishes markedly.

NEWSLETTERS: GETTING EASIER TO PRODUCE

George Columbo, president of Influence Technologies in Winter Springs, Florida, is a staunch believer in newsletters. "Imagine being able to sit with each of your clients once a month to have an extended conversation about ways your business can help theirs," Columbo says. "You could highlight your technical expertise, help them understand system and software options, and remind them that yours is the company to call for help. You could also tell them about the latest products, special offers, or promotions."

Most marketers gravitate toward marketing techniques designed to generate new business, and that's certainly important. As your business progresses beyond the early years, however, you need to concentrate on cultivating repeat business from existing clients.

A newsletter can help position you as a value-added, service-oriented company. Informative articles about emerging technologies or stories about how other clients use technology demonstrate that your business is a market leader.

"A newsletter can also help your business sell add-on products and services," Columbo says. If you're like most marketers, your sales people probably have an unfortunate tendency to fixate on the matters at hand. As a result, clients never learn about other products and services.

Many marketers find newsletters particularly effective for selling training and software upgrades. One manufacturer features in-depth articles about product upgrades before they are released. On the day of release, he has a backlog of orders waiting to be filled!

"Don't create a newsletter that reads like an advertorial or infomercial," Columbo warns. "If it's perceived as such, it will cease to work as a sales tool." If it's perceived as a value-added service, then it can be one of the most powerful marketing tools in your arsenal.

Service professionals we know who use newsletters for marketing are amazed at the results. Some report that if a newsletter is a few days late, clients call wondering where it is. Not a bad response, eh?

A Targeted, Tasteful Document

While your newsletter may directly generate new business, like all of the other marketing tools discussed, it is part of a client-centered marketing system that favorably and continuously keeps your name in front of those people who can reward you with new business or speak favorably about you to others.

The newsletter is a particularly effective print-related promotion vehicle in support of your prospecting efforts (see Chapter 27). While you may not be able to call continuously on all prospective clients as frequently as you would like, once a legitimate prospect has been identified, the newsletter enables you to maintain contact—beneficial for converting prospects to clients in the future.

Developing Regular Features

Whether you are issuing your first newsletter or your fiftieth, the development of regular features will help to decrease the problem of what to include. Each of the following may contribute to the information, education, and promotion functions of your newsletter:

- *Message from the president, branch, or managing partner.* This message could reflect trends in the targets' industry since the last newsletter, mixed with personal opinion, forecasts, or other observations.

- *Capitol Roundup.* Provide information on current or proposed legis-lation, new rules, or regulations that may impact clients. If your practice area is national in scope, you will find that many clients appreciate getting the early word on these developments.

- *Client of the Month.* Profile one of your clients, particularly featur-ing something the client has done that represents bold, progressive, or insightful thinking. You will make 12 good friends in this com-ing year by establishing this column—the 12 clients featured.

- *Industry Calendar of Events.* List the important meetings, seminars, conventions, and symposiums of interest to members of your target niche. This kind of data is often derived from other publications; nevertheless, recipients will appreciate having it listed concisely in your newsletter.

- *Technical Report.* Offer a roundup of new equipment or technology that supports clients' efforts. Your assessment of the effectiveness of new equipment, costs, and potential applications will be appreci-ated by many recipients.

- *Interview.* Present a 150- to 300-word interview with principals of your firm; movers and shakers in the industry; association execu-tives; magazine, journal, or newsletter publishers in the industry; key clients and client staff people; and other outside experts. The interview—in question-and-answer format—provides a visual break from normal text layouts.

- *Reprints, excerpts, and adaptations.* Reprint information that first ap-peared in another print medium. You will have to secure permis-sion, which in most cases is readily granted.

System Maintenance

Each issue of the newsletter must be assessed for balance, readabil-ity, and adherence to the firm's goals and objectives in producing the newsletter in the first place. A newsletter that accurately conveys your firm's goals and objectives is a marketing tool worth maintaining.

Generally, one person must be responsible for its publication and distribution, though others will have input. One- and three-page newsletters are possible, but have drawbacks. A one-page newsletter doesn't allow much depth of coverage of topics or features—clients and recipients may not save the issues. A three-page newsletter—three sin-gle sheets joined by a staple, or two sheets folded over to make four normal-sized pages with the back sheet for mailing—appears a bit unbalanced.

Two-, four-, and six-page newsletters are popular. Two pages (front and back) or four pages (two 11"×17" pages folded over) are simple in design and easy to mail. A six-pager, which equals a four-pager with insert, is a popular option. At the eight- or ten-page level, you have to consider the difficulty in maintaining reader interest.

Many direct mail and newsletter pros suggest having your newsletter three-hole punched to encourage recipients to save them. The most popular page size in the United States remains $8^1/_2" \times 11"$. A larger page doesn't fit into notebooks or file folders. A smaller page may get lost among other documents.

AN ALTERNATIVE: INFORMATION BOOKLETS

An educational flyer or brochure is also a useful tool to generate publicity. Many organizations, such as professional and industrial trade associations, produce generic industry literature. At the individual firm level, successful firms have produced printed material with titles such as:

- Eight Things to Look For in Selecting an Attorney.
- Five Services Your Accountant Should Be Providing.
- How a Management Consultant Can Help You.

Notice that these are not titles that highlight the specific benefits of your own services. Rather, they provide general education about the profession, with the implication being that since your firm is aware of such criteria, you also meet the criteria. The educational flyer can readily be converted into an article with a minimum of effort.

USE SOMEONE ELSE'S ARTICLE

Finally, consider using an article written by someone else (in which you're not mentioned). If you wish to make an important point to a client, use data, quotes, or studies that support your proposal or service suggestion. For instance, a consultant obtained permission to duplicate an article that summarized the eight key factors found in successful organizations by Peters and Waterman. The consultant sent an accompanying letter to prospects that said, "I disagree with two of the factors discussed in the article and have discovered another factor not identified by the authors. I'll call you next week to see if you would like to discuss your situation and receive a brief description of the 'ninth factor.' "

Getting articles published will serve to supplement a good marketing program but will not, by any means, replace it. Also, the positive effects of getting an article published are largely temporary. However, in combination with the effective use of other marketing tools, a published article can provide useful benefits, indeed.

CHAPTER 24

Tapping the Local Press

An effective method of marketing and promoting your professional practice is through the use of publicity and public relations.

Public relations work basically means disseminating information via articles, fact sheets, press releases, media advisories, press conferences, and media tours to obtain favorable coverage.

Used properly, publicity can function much like paid advertising, sometimes even better. It builds audience awareness and enhances public opinion of you and your products—two surefire ingredients for growing sales.

A key difference, however, between public relations and advertising is that P.R. is generated by a neutral third party, the media. Therefore, publicity generated this way tends to deliver something that paid advertising generally doesn't, namely believability.

That's the beauty of P.R. That's why leaders of industry make it a priority. Bill Gates keeps people talking about his products because he keeps the Microsoft name in front of the buying public.

Fortunately for the small practitioner, the generation of publicity does not require substantial time or effort. What is required is familiarity with techniques designed to generate publicity and implementation of those techniques with which you feel comfortable.

In this chapter, you'll learn:

☐ What publicity is.

☐ What a news release is.

☐ Who can submit news releases.

☐ Good topics for news releases.

☐ Other techniques for using the local press.

PUBLICIZE, PUBLICIZE

For many professionals a sustained advertising campaign is beyond the resources of the firm. Through an effective public relations campaign and the generation of publicity, however, it is possible to use media sources, particularly the local press, to keep your name in front of targets of opportunity.

Public relations involves all planned activities undertaken to influence public opinion. Publicity is a key component of public relations and has been defined as media coverage of events, including background information, descriptions, relevant data, or other current information involving an individual, product (or service), business, or organization.

It's not always more costly and difficult to get an article written and placed than to simply take out an ad. The cost of getting an article written, which may span several pages and include photos, is likely to be far less than a single-page ad in the same publication. While the advance planning, coordination, and acceptance of the self-generated article require considerable effort, it is a very sound investment. A well-placed article in a widely read publication can have a greater impact than an entire year's worth of advertisements.

NEWS RELEASES TO MEDIA

There are, of course, far less expensive ways to gain publicity. You can submit a news release—that is, information about your firm—to newspapers and radio at no cost and obtain free publicity. Some of the items that make good press releases include promotions of individuals within the firm, the hiring of new personnel, where you will be speaking, contract awards received, relocation or renovation of your offices, results of surveys you've completed, and expansion of your services. Each of these items is sufficient information to make a good news release. A more comprehensive list of news release topics is presented in Figure 24–1.

Read your local newspaper today and you likely will spot two or

FIGURE 24-1
Good Topics for News Releases

Services
New clients.
Studies you've completed.
Office expansion, renovation,
     relocation.
New service introduction.
New uses for existing products.
Lower cost due to more efficient
     operation.
Services that address newsworthy topics.
Unusual service offerings.
Bids or awards.
New contracts.

Firm
Affiliations.
Equipment installations.
Accomplishments.
Mergers, acquisitions.
Anniversaries of firm, principals,
     or long-term employees.
Association memberships.
New building or radical change
     in office layout.
Banquets or awards dinners.
Employee training programs.
Projected plans.
Joint programs—government,
     industry.

Promotion
Special distinction.
Contests, new offers, premiums.
Exhibits, trade shows, displays.
Promotion success story.
Visits by notable individuals.
Overcoming competitors.
New design, trademark, logo.
New market areas—industry,
     geography.

Employees
Speaking engagements.
Reprints of speeches.
Travel abroad.
Interesting backgrounds, hobbies.
Noteworthy accomplishments.
Increase in employee benefits.
Employee awards.
Retirements, births, deaths.
Civic activities.
Courses completed, certificates,
     citations, degrees, licenses.
Seminars attended.
Software developed.
Publications—books, articles.
Cassettes, videos produced.

Community Activity
Fund-raising events.
Program sponsorship, i.e.,
     scholarships to foreign
     exchange students, internships.
Memorial, dedication, or testimonial
     ceremonies.
Training community labor force.
Local news that relates to
     company.
Community exhibits in which
     company has taken part.
Local election to office of
     company official.
Meeting announcements.

Research
Survey results.
New discoveries.
Trends, projections, forecasts.
New equipment or facility
     development.

three news releases about professionals in your area. The releases will state the names of the firm, the locations, what they do, and probably quotes from the principals.

There is nothing complicated about getting great press coverage. First, you need a story that is interesting to the publication's readers. Second, it must conform to the style of the publication. Third, it must reach the right editor.

Okay, so you have a good story, the first requirement. Then, customize each press release to a corresponding publication, the second requirement. To complete the three-point process, call the editors of each publication. Briefly explain what you do and what you've accomplished.

Then comes the most important part: Ask each editor for a few minutes of help in preparing the press release for the publication. What did the editor think of the story? What could be done to improve it? What kind of format, deadline, and so on does the editor consider in choosing press releases for publication?

Not surprisingly, many editors are usually supportive, helpful, and interested. They help you target their individual needs.

Formal press releases from relative unknowns tend to get lost in the impersonal deluge of press releases that publications receive every month. On the other hand, letters or other personally addressed correspondence are much more likely to be considered.

Unlike ads or sales literature, press releases must appear objective and newsworthy, so don't use superlatives. Like any other marketing document, however, make sure they look and sound professional. Even if you need an outside writer, press releases can be your most cost-effective marketing tool. A sample news release is provided in Figure 24–2.

NEWS RELEASE FOLLOW-UP

After submitting your news release, you should undertake the following activities:

News Release Follow-Up

It's no typographical error; after you submit a news release to an editor, do nothing. If your release is run, you'll know soon enough. Your associ-

FIGURE 24–2
Sample News Release

George Franks and Company
West Haven Professional Building
Pasadena, California 99999
(818) 888-8888
Fax: 888-7777
E-mail: george@gfc.com

FOR IMMEDIATE RELEASE
Contact: Sue Powell
888-8888

PASADENA ARCHITECT EXPANDS OFFICE

George Franks and Company, an architectural firm practicing in the Pasadena area for the past four years, recently moved its office to the West Haven Professional Building located near the courthouse downtown.

"This new office," said George Franks, "will enable us to increase both our staff and the range of services provided." In addition, the location is easily accessible by public transportation.

Franks, who first began his practice in Pasadena on King Street in 1988 with a staff of two, now employs a staff of 12, including four junior partners and a full-time editor/production coordinator. The new office, located on the second floor of the Professional Building, occupies 3600 square feet.

"In the last year and a half it became apparent that our old office had simply become too small and that we could not provide the level of service our clients were accustomed to," Franks said. Franks is a member of the California State Society of Architects and the American Institute of Architecture.

---

ates, friends, and relatives will be calling! However, it is *not* wise or recommended that you:

Call the editor.	Leave messages for the editor.
Ask for clippings.	Visit the editor.
Seek a publication date.	Do anything but wait.

Your release, if used, is printed based on the newspaper's needs, availability of space, prominence of you and your firm, and a host of other factors already at play. Any contact that you attempt to make after submitting a release is usually perceived as an irritation to the editor. "So write 'em, send 'em, and relax!"

PUBLIC "THANK YOU" MESSAGES

Another way to generate publicity is through a public thank-you message. This method has been used successfully many times. It is not perceived as an advertisement (although you must pay for it just as you do for advertising). The objective is to draw attention to your firm by showing appreciation for your clients.

The way to do this is to place an ad, usually in the local news or business section of the newspaper, stating that your firm "wishes to thank its 100 (or the appropriate number) clients for letting us help you with your hopes and dreams. May your coming years be as profitable as the ones that have passed." Variations of this message will also be effective. You then list the name, address, and telephone number of your firm. This message has been known to bring in many calls, and because it does not appear to be advertising, you maintain a low-key, professional image. A sample is presented in Figure 24–3.

LETTERS TO THE EDITOR

To enhance your firm's image and build a positive awareness, you need to identify and capitalize on any other available publicity opportunities, such as writing letters to the editor and opinion pieces.

FIGURE 24–3
Sample Public Thank-You Notice

Ronald DeVries and Company
Consulting Engineers
Brussels
Wishes its 150 clients a very
Merry Christmas. Thanks
for sharing your
dreams with us.
May next year
be your best.

Letters to the editor, particularly in response to controversial issues, generate more exposure than most people realize. The magazines, journals, and newsletters in the niche are read eagerly by its members. A reply to the editor or an editorial opinion that reflects your understanding of the niche has a significant impact. Don't hesitate to be controversial if you have a strong and well-founded view. A published letter to the editor in one of your professional journals can be used for marketing purposes when an attractive reprint of the letter, including the date, page, and logo of the publication in which it is contained, is included with your correspondence to clients and prospects (much as you would use an article). In fact, a well-written letter to the editor, regardless of the publication in which it appears, in many instances, can serve as an adequate substitute to writing a full-blown article.

The letter to the editor registers a distinct impact with those who read it. It positions you as a responsible, authoritative professional who is taking a leadership and advocacy position on what is presumably an important, current topic.

Some guidelines for submitting letters to the editor are presented in Figure 24–4.

The reading public, which may include many of the people you wish to serve, often finds it easier and more interesting to read letters to the editor than articles appearing in the same publication. Because of the single-column, unintimidating appearance of such letters, many people do not hesitate to read one after another.

The key to getting a letter to the editor published in your local

FIGURE 24–4
Submitting Letters to the Editor

Type your letter, keeping it short and to the point.

Include your name, affiliation, address, and all telephone numbers (the editor may call you to verify that it was in fact you who sent the letter, or to obtain clarification).

Provide the editor with a title or prelude to your letter, i.e., "In Response to Your Article on XYZ . . ." or "On the Issue of UVW . . ."

Avoid accusative, rhetorical, or cynical overtones.

Suggest a solution, if possible, to the issue or problem to which you have alluded.

newspaper—other than submitting an excellent letter—is speed. Call up the publication in question, inform them that you have a letter to the editor that you would like to send by fax, and obtain their fax number. The editor in charge of the letter page will appreciate the quick response and, now and then, will even call you back within 24 hours. Generally, however, your local newspaper receives all the letters it can handle and must select a few from a wide field. So, don't be disappointed if yours is not chosen.

Whereas the competition to get into your local paper may be significant, professional, trade, and industry magazines and journals often go begging when it comes to obtaining poignant, thought-provoking letters. As with other articles and news releases, send your letters to more than one publication. If your local newspaper and a professional journal both want to print the letter, you will have no problem. If two professional journals wish to print the same letter, then you must withdraw your letter from one of the publications.

CHAPTER 25

Leveraging Your Memberships in the Niche's Organizations

Visit any metropolitan area and attend a local meeting of the Red Cross, International Rotary, Les Femmes Chefs D'Entreprises Mondiale, or other civic, professional, or charitable groups, and undoubtedly you will meet many of the area's most successful professionals. Successful professionals know that giving of their time freely is an excellent way to be of service to the community and to help build the firm.

After completing this chapter, you'll know:

☐ Why it is important to join charitable and civic organizations.

☐ The names of at least three national groups that have chapters in your area.

☐ The key reason for joining an organization.

☐ Why joining any organization will be fruitless if you do not meet and remember targets of opportunity and influence.

☐ The two best leadership positions to hold in any organization.

EARNING A POSITION OF LEADERSHIP

Civic organizations, such as the chamber of commerce, Scouts, and the YMCA, afford professionals ample opportunity to rub elbows with key community and business leaders and jointly work on solving local, civic, public, and business problems. In marketing your professional services, it is often assumed that you are fully competent in your practice area. The important thing is getting known throughout the community and getting known among your peer group in other professions. Earning a position of leadership in a high-visibility organization is an excellent way to be of service and, as a by-product, promote your services. By volunteering your services and assisting civic and charitable organizations, targets of opportunity and influence come to know you as a person and then feel comfortable in using you as a professional or in referring your services to others.

Joining and serving can only be effective if you pay the price required to gain a leadership position in the organizations and associations in which your *targets* belong. You are leveraging off the reputation of the organization and the lead time necessary to begin to receive benefits can range from 6 to 18 months. Many professionals don't stand their ground; they drop out and never realize that benefits of leveraging were just around the corner.

An unsophisticated marketer joined an organization and unrealistically expected to generate new business simply as a result of attending various meetings and becoming known. After nearly two years, he resigned his membership and concluded that joining organizations "just isn't for me."

A resourceful consultant joined an organization comprised of decision makers in her targeted prospective client organizations. She sought and was appointed to the new member committee. Serving in this capacity, she met all new members, and during the course of the screening, interviews, and subsequent new member activities, developed sound relationships that eventually led to opportunities to discuss ways of serving them.

Later, she was appointed to the program development committee. While serving in this capacity, she contacted the community's leading speakers to determine if they would speak to the organization. Within a year, she had first-name acquaintance with several community influentials.

JOINING TO SERVE WITH A PURPOSE

Memberships in professional and civic activities need to be closely monitored to determine whether marketing results in addition to personal satisfaction are being achieved. Otherwise, joining can be a serious drain on the firm in terms of time and energy. Because every community is different, and the interplay of political, social, cultural, and religious spheres varies from time to time, a customized joining-serving strategy must be prepared.

It is essential for professionals to continually analyze organizational contacts for relationships that should be developed, paying particular attention to younger executives on their way up. This approach must be balanced, however, with the realization that the only organizations that one should join are those in which one has a genuine interest and desire to serve.

Numerous strategies abound for the successful penetration of charitable and civic organizations. One way is to seek specific offices. For example, the role of activities chairman is a coveted position in many groups because one can gain a high degree of visibility and have virtually unlimited access to key people in one's market and practice area.

If there are two or three or more partners in your firm, you can match partners' personal interests with the firm's goals. Thus, Jones may join A, B, and C groups, whereas Brown joins D, E, and F. You may choose to join C, F, and G, thereby increasing your firm's visibility in organizations C and F and maintaining some visibility in all seven groups.

If you do not meet and remember targets of opportunity and influence, and they do not remember you, the act of joining any organization will be fruitless from a marketing standpoint. Some professionals maintain card files on individuals when a key contact is made. Information is continuously added to the card file as it is obtained.

Making targets of opportunity and influence remember you is a delicate matter. The best way is to respond professionally and completely when asked about your profession and not to oversell. If your commitment to and involvement with a charitable or civic association is extensive, you may rightly expect that you will become known and remembered by many of the right people.

Figure 25–1 is an example of how an accounting firm in Calgary formalized community involvement among its professional staff.

FIGURE 25–1
Sample Community Involvement Planning Form

West District Office *Community Involvement Plans* *Period from _____ to _____*		
Name of Organization	*Date Joined*	*Number of* *Meetings*

DO THEY USE YOUR SERVICE?

The most effective technique in joining with a purpose is to seek out that group whose members routinely use your type of service. Marilyn Coopman offers management training seminars. Using Gale's *Encyclopedia of Associations*, she identified a group called Meeting Planners

Describe Your Plans to Become Active in the Organization. Include Committees, Offices, etc. and Expected Time Frame	Estimated Time Reqirements

International. She called them long distance and found that Meeting Planners International had a chapter in her city. She obtained membership information from the national headquarters, and then made contact and ultimately joined the local chapter.

Marilyn discovered that she did not have to be a meeting planner herself in order to join the association. She joined in an associate capacity. Many types of associations maintain different categories of membership. This greatly increases their membership rolls and provides a service for members who then are in a position to interact with potential suppliers and service providers.

Over the next year, Marilyn faithfully attended sessions, volunteered to serve on committees, and at one monthly meeting was featured

FIGURE 25–2
Volunteer Groups

Audubon Society.	Labor Party.
Boys' Club.	Lions.
Business and Professional Women's Club.	March of Dimes.
	Masons.
Cancer Society.	Optimist Club.
Catholic Youth Organization.	Parent-Teacher Association.
Chamber of commerce.	Public Television.
Children's Hospital committees.	Regional park authority.
Civitan.	Republican Party.
Conservative Party.	Rotary Club International.
Democratic Party.	Salvation Army.
Easter Seal campaign.	SCORE (Service Corps of Retired Executives).
Elks.	
Explorers.	Scouts.
Fraternities (professional).	Sierra Club.
Garden club.	Sertomas.
Goodwill Industries.	Special Olympics.
Green Political Party.	Toastmasters International.
Heart Fund.	United Way.
Historical society.	United We Stand (reform party).
Independent Party.	Volunteer services.
Jaycees.	Walkathons.
Jewish community center.	Wilderness Society.
Junior chamber of commerce.	YMCA, YWCA.
Kiwanis.	Zontas.

herself. Because the members of the local MPI chapter began to know her and were impressed with her presentation, she received several phone calls from meeting planners (members) who were interested in having her present one of her seminars within their respective organizations.

Robert Zyblut, a diversified financial services broker for an internationally recognized brokerage firm, volunteered to chair a suburban Maryland society of certified public accountants. Each month, Robert identified and secured a speaker for the group; wrote, edited, and distributed a newsletter; and became a one-man information clearinghouse.

As you might guess, many of the CPAs retained Robert as a counselor for their personal investments and referred others to him. Though his time and commitment to this group were substantial, Robert found

FIGURE 25-3
Suggested Types of Organizations by Staff and Executive Level

1. Engagement Staff:
   - Alumni organizations.
   - Professional societies such as state societies of CPAs.
2. Engagement Supervisor:
   - Alumni organizations.
   - Professional societies.
   - Civic groups (e.g., junior chamber of commerce).
3. Manager:
   - Business/trade associations (e.g., American Bankers Association, chamber of commerce).
   - Professional societies (e.g., Planning Executives Institute).
4. Partner:
   - Business/trade organizations.
   - Civic groups.
   - Charitable organizations (e.g., United Way).
   - Cultural groups such as art society or symphony.
   - Community-oriented organizations (e.g., school board, American Red Cross).
   - Luncheon club.
   - Country club.

that on balance he had generated more new clients in a shorter time period than in his entire professional career.

GROUPS, ANYONE?

Why not take the time right now to identify six organizations in your community that interest you? The list in Figure 25–2 offers the names of groups that may commonly be found in your area. A local phone call will yield membership information. Figure 25–3 lists kinds of groups suitable for staff and executives.

CHAPTER 26

Expanding Services to Current Clients

This chapter builds directly upon what you learned in two previous chapters. In Chapter 9, "Managing Your Targets of Opportunity," you learned the importance of indicating potential problems and highlighting opportunity areas that you encountered for the attention of the client contact person. You also looked at ways to build marketing into the engagement process.

In Chapter 16, "Building Marketing into the Fabric of the Firm," you learned about the importance of building client-centered marketing into the engagement process. The present chapter extends this knowledge and focuses on further expanding your services to your current clients.

Upon completing the chapter you will:

☐ Identify extensions or add-ons to the present engagement.

☐ Employ first engagement strategies.

☐ Gain tips for maintaining communications between engagements.

SATISFYING CLIENTS IS YOUR FIRST ORDER OF BUSINESS

Existing clients, if properly managed, represent your private, captive market. You've earned the right to be heard regarding ideas for improving their performance. If you fail to fully serve a client, there is a strong probability that the client will go outside and get additional services that you could have provided. This weakens the relationship and threatens existing revenue sources. Hence, smart marketers make sensing, serving, and satisfying the needs of their desirable, high-potential clients their first order of business. What does this entail?

1. Identifying both short-term and long-term opportunities based upon your awareness of client needs and operations and your evaluation of the services (yours and other firms') at present employed by the client.

2. Providing additional profitable services to receptive existing clients with known or suspected needs. Identifying the resources they may be willing to invest or can be induced to invest in your proposed client-centered service solution.

3. Enhancing relationships at all levels to lay the groundwork for any additional services that are needed and demonstrating your continued interest in the client.

Your Continuing Opportunities

Almost independent of the situation, you can seek to offer extensions to services you're currently providing by expanding the scope of work to be done (i.e., you initiate the idea of expanding the scope of the work during your present engagement). For example, Dick was engaged to produce an organization plan for the marketing department of a services firm. During the engagement, Dick planted the "seed of need" regarding the importance of taking the ideas to the actual how-to level. The result was an extension of the scope of Dick's work to include the prepararion of position responsibilities along with a two-day training program.

In a nutshell, strive to:

- Continually build trust and confidence with the client.

- Spot unmet needs, always starting by looking for leads on present project.

- Bring identified needs to the attention of management during current project.

- Educate them as to the value of addressing the issues now.

- Be on the alert for new need areas between projects as well.

EMPLOYING CURRENT ENGAGEMENT ACTIONS

If you don't have many clients at present, or you're new in business, you may be relieved to know that even your *first* or present engagement offers you many opportunities for providing additional services.

Having frequent contact with the decision making unit (DMU) players: During any engagement, the key is looking for leads in all the right places. As with any new connection, frequent and sensitive communications help build the underpinning of the relationship. Keep your contacts informed! Frequent contact also enables you to handle any postsale buyer remorse, or attempts to change the agreed-upon scope of the work.

Presenting early, visible results: In first engagement situations, it's a good idea to structure your work so that you can present results early and often. When the client sees results early and often (but not to the point of excess), it makes the DMU players feel more confident. From their perspective every outside service professional they bring in is a risk, at least in the beginning. Hence, they often wonder if they have made a good investment. Showing them results by, say, Day Two helps.

Conducting an end-of-the-engagement satisfaction meeting: The optimal satisfaction meeting includes all of the DMU players and client contact persons—everyone involved in the preparation, promotion, performance, and perfection of the service you've provided. (Also see the engagement wrap-up section of Chapter 16.)

MAINTAINING COMMUNICATIONS BETWEEN ENGAGEMENTS

"I've been thinking of you." What a nice message when it comes from someone who successfully served you in the past. You want to offer the same type of message whether in the form of a letter or a phone call (fax and E-mail don't quite cut it here). At least once quarterly, all non-current clients should receive either a letter or a call from you.

CHAPTER 27

Prospecting for High-Potential New Clients

Prospecting refers to the activities involved in finding and contacting qualified suspects to obtain appointments to discuss solutions for a known or suspected need. Prospecting has been called "the search for needers who can be changed first into wanters, and then into buyers."

After completing this chapter you will:

☐ Know the differences among the three types of prospecting.

☐ See why client-centered prospecting is a superior approach to prospecting.

☐ Learn achievable prospecting objectives.

☐ Know the subtleties between prospecting in geographic and cyberspace markets.

THE THREE TYPES OF PROSPECTING

The notion of prospecting has evolved over the years. Figure 27–1 describes the differences among the three types of prospecting.

FIGURE 27–1
Three Types of Prospecting

Traditional Prospecting

"Let me tell you about our company: its services, products, and people. I know more about what I do than you do. My job is telling you about my company so you can figure out how and where to use our services."

Consultative Prospecting

"I see my job as using my questioning and listening skills to learn more about you. I ask you to invest your time and share information about your company and operations so I can figure out the needs you have that I can meet with my capabilities. When you open your 'corporate kimono' to me I'll make recommendations that include my services."

Client-Centered Prospecting

"I see my job as proactively sharing my insider's knowledge of success factors, and proposing a value-adding solution program designed to enable you to be better at some aspect of your business. I know about your company, its operations and the success requirements you have. I know the business conditions that are driving the marketing needs in your business and markets. I've accumulated and codified my experience in your niche and have distilled it into action programs designed to increase your profit, reduce your costs, and increase your productivity."

As you read over the statements that characterize the essence of each of the three approaches, consider these questions: Whom do clients and prospects want to deal with in today's business environment? What type of prospecting do you think is going to be highly wasteful, frustrating, and demoralizing? In what type of prospecting will your firm engage?

THE FOUR CRITERIA OF A TRUE PROSPECT

You can hunt for prospects to the far ends of the earth, Biosphere 2, and even Space Lab; however, to efficiently prospect, it makes sense to understand who, in fact, fits the bill.

1. True prospects have a need, and you can make them see that their need is important enough to have you solve it. Simply having a need isn't enough if there is no chance for you to be heard, let alone understood and heeded.

2. True prospects have sufficient financial resources to do what is required to solve the need. Having a need but no funds to meet the need leads to trouble if you land such a party as a client. Do you recognize any of your "D" clients?

3. True prospects can be induced to invest the resources. In short, they can be persuaded to see that it makes more sense to part with some resources and take care of the need situation than to retain said resources and ignore the need situation.

4. True prospects represent those with whom you can work to make the solution a reality.

THREE PROSPECTING ACCOMPLISHMENTS

Entire books have been written about prospecting, so one chapter, at best, can present the best of the best. Realistically, what can you accomplish if you're starting or revamping the prospecting process in your firm? Basically, there are three accomplishments that are both attainable and sustainable.

Continually Generate a Sufficient Number of Qualified Leads

You lose clients for a variety of reasons. Some clients are not fun to serve, and thus, you fire them. Or perhaps it's because you have provided a one-time-only service. Perhaps they've left the area, have been absorbed, or have chosen to broaden their mix of suppliers for your type of service. Regardless, more often than most service providers would care to admit, generating a sufficient number of qualified new leads is vital to the overall health and well-being of your firm.

Use Prospecting to Further the Strategic Goals of Your Organization

Changing business conditions can often force you to change the nature and mix of clients to seek and serve. Hence, the nature and mix of clients you serve at present are testimony to the type of prospects you sought yesterday. The type of prospects you generate today will define, to a greater or lesser degree, the nature of your business tomorrow.

Design and Install a Client-Centered Prospecting Program

Engaging in client-centered prospecting enables you to work within your comfort zone, maximize your marketing efforts, and minimize the time and effort required to keep your potential new-business pipeline flowing. You feel better about prospecting in general and hence do it more often and with more energy.

TWO MAJOR TASKS

There are two major tasks involved in successful prospecting endeavors: (1) building an administrative structure that goads and guides you, and (2) designing targeted prospecting campaigns for use in your geographical and cyberspace markets.

Building the Administrative Structure

To build the administrative structure necessary to conduct and manage a successful, ongoing prospecting campaign, you can now draw upon the data you've already assembled in Chapter 5. Please refer to Figure 5–1, Current Prospects Work Sheet.

Remember that your current prospects and suspects lists are valuable assets. The number and quality of your current prospects and suspects largely determine the strength and well-being of your practice.

The additional data you may want to generate to keep abreast of your firm's prospecting activities doesn't need to be extremely complex. Three useful and highly revealing items to track include:

1. *Open leads:* a list of suspects to contact who have been prequalified by means of a lead from a referral source.

2. *Proposals issued:* a list of proposals outstanding by date issued, prospect name, potential fees, and the like.

3. *Performance metrics:* a record of your cumulative success ratio.

Designing Prospecting Campaigns in Geographic Markets

You can aim your prospecting campaign toward geographic or cyberspace markets. We'll tackle geographic markets first.

Your goal is finding new suspects and obtaining appointments to discuss a need situation with a decision maker in the organization. This involves several steps:

1. *Set goals for a prospecting direct mail campaign.* Among various goals you can select are:

   - To send out a certain number of packages per week, per staff person, or within a niche.

   - To enclose only the most recent articles with hot-button needs.

   - To have one in 20 recipients call (this would be fabulous).

   - To have people recall receiving your package when you call.

   - To eventually land X percent appointments.

2. *Select the hot-button need to be promoted.* Select a need that is really hot in that it is current, important, and detrimental to the continued well-being of the prospect organization if it's not handled. By identifying hot-button or recurring needs to use when making initial contact with suspects, you will increase the probability of obtaining an appointment, thus minimizing the number of false starts. It is time-consuming and mentally and emotionally draining to call on nonreceptive, uninterested targets.

   In contrast, busy decision-makers are interested in discussing a need situation, especially if they think some free information enabling them to do the job themselves can be obtained. When calling them to discuss a hot button, you have already answered the foremost question in their minds, "What can I gain from talking to you?"

3. *Select suspects for a campaign.* Now is when you'll be glad that you did the work required to build the list of suspects for contact. Re-

FIGURE 27–2
Preparing the Initial-Contact Mailing Package

The package you mail to the targeted suspect contains two pieces:

1. An enclosure—an article or abridgment of a study or report dealing with a hot-button need of the party to whom you're sending the package. The enclosure underscores the importance of the need and helps you make your selling point.

2. A cover letter that triggers one or more buying motives and interests the recipient in meeting with you to discuss the value-adding solution approach.

To prepare the enclosure:

1. Find an article, preferably one appearing in a publication serving the niche, which discusses the hot-button need you want to highlight and for which you have a solution. The article should give you the basis for discussing a solution in your accompanying letter (see below). It's best to use an article that copies or scans well, with insets, sidebars, and graphics.

2. Contact the publisher to obtain reprint rights. Ask permission to reuse it on a limited and nonsale basis. Don't photocopy the article or article abridgment; that would convey the perception of your "going cheap"—an image that you can't afford.

3. Highlight paragraphs and sections that make your selling point for you.

To prepare the cover letter:

1. A good letter gets right to the point and tells why a meeting with the sender will be beneficial to the receiver. To increase the probability that your letter has impact, base the body of the letter on a variation of the AIDA format discussed in Chapter 2.

2. AIDA, applied to letters:

   Attention. In the opening paragraph or sentence, mention a strong benefit to the reader.

   Interest. Your letter must stress how your service solution will enable the reader to better do what the person is in business to do.

   Desire. Tactfully mention that the reader lacks the benefits you can provide, and these benefits can be discussed at a meeting with you. Offer compelling reasons for meeting with you when you call for an appointment.

   Affirmation. In the letter, put the date that you intend to call the contact.

member, your goal is to target only those organizations and individuals that are most likely to have the need you are promoting, want the need to be solved now, and have the funds necessary to make it happen.

4. *Prepare the initial-contact mailing package.* Figure 27–2 describes the two major parts of the initial-contact mailing package—the need-specific enclosure and the cover letter.

5. *Market-test the campaign.* Select 10 to 15 suspects for a test mailing. Mail your package to the test suspects and then call for an appointment. Using a prepared guide or telescript is suggested. No matter how well-versed you or your staff may be in using the phone, there's too much at stake for you to work without a script. At the very least, the script will remind you of important points to make. At the most, the script will provide a reliable fallback if or when you lose your train of thought or your place the discussion.

Attempt to schedule an appointment with the prospect to discuss the mailing. Regardless of your success in this market-test step, the end product is a fine-tuning of the package and the telescript.

6. *Continue the campaign.* Now you have tested the package and sharpened your phone technique, so let 'er rip. Continue the campaign by mailing to the remaining suspects. Jeff finds that 10 to 15 packages per week with follow-up is about the most you can and need to take on. All the while be cognizant that:

- People respond to other people.
- Recipients prefer that you get right to the point.
- Your suggestions need to be specific and actionable.
- Prospects are seeking guidance and direction.

Prospecting in Cyberspace

Is it easy for people to find your Web page? Once there, do visitors find your Web page to be sufficiently stimulating to want to contact you via E-mail, hence enabling you to quickly respond to their expressions of interest?

When it comes to Web sites, you have to give to get—you have to provide value to hook the visitor and then encourage the individual to reach for you. It's essential that you are clear about your offer. For example, Dick wasted a lot of time at first because his marketing coach page did not clearly state that the advice was at a cost to the visitor. After he made this point clear, the number of E-mail messages he received dropped substantially. Many times the best that a Web page does for you is to build name awareness.

Jeff's Web page (http://www.BreathingSpace.com) attracted a lot of one-time visitors before he decided to offer a "Breathing Space" tip sheet changed every Monday (52 annually!). He also added a bonus giveaway in his section on the scores of books reviewed from a Breathing Space perspective. Now, any visitor can request the first review for free and receive it via E-mail or fax.

A Web site is like an on-line brochure, a marketing statement. To design your Web page to generate prospects, make the page sufficiently interesting for visitors to want to spend their precious time there and sufficiently intriguing for them to want to send you an E-mail inquiry.

The page obviously needs to be attractive. Few visitors will invest time in waiting for a graphic image download, especially if they are visiting the page for the first time. If you're going to feature long pages of text and material, then offer visitors convenient frames or links so that they can intuitively and speedily move around your site. *Internet World*, a monthly magazine available via snail mail, offers a wealth of information on designing effective Web sites.

Be sure to list your site with the major browsing services and search engines. For a convenient list of major search tools visit http://www.albany.net/allinone or http://www.search.com, among other sites.

Go ahead and establish a response memo to capitalize on the E-mail inquiry, and investigate the automatic bounce-back program that many consultants are building. Such programs enable you to automatically field inquiries while giving you a comprehensive summary of what you received and sent, on demand. At all times, your goal in prospecting via the Web is to rapidly respond to an inquiry in an interesting manner that encourages the visitor to entertain doing business with you.

CHAPTER 28

Selling the Value-Adding Solution

Client-centered selling involves tailoring solutions for client satisfaction. This chapter focuses on helping you to plan and conduct effective new-business meetings and to discuss your proposed solution to a recognized hot-button need of the prospect.

In geographic markets, selling refers to the face-to-face meetings with one or more members of a suspect's organization. In cyberspace, your selling opportunity is driven by the visitor's inquiry. For example, a growing number of professionals provide cyberspace services via E-mail—such as consulting, critiquing marketing materials, reviewing proposals, editing, and providing technical instruction—to clients that have never been met face-to-face. Under this scenario, the selling is really a form of order-taking following a relatively brief exchange of information regarding the service provider's billing approach.

After reading the chapter and absorbing the practical materials, you will be able to:

☐ Prepare for an effective new-business meeting.

☐ Employ a logical approach to selling new business.

☐ Advance your personal sales capability measurably.

To be good at selling your value-added solutions, you only need to master handling premeeting tasks, guiding the meeting, and handling postmeeting tasks. While these phases have to be carefully planned for and executed, you can keep all activities well within your comfort zone. Let's tackle them in order.

THE PREMEETING PREPARATION PHASE

There are three major activities in this phase—nonarduous:

Preparing an interview guide will make everything go smoother. The guide will outline the points you need to make, and identify the information you need to verify and obtain.

Preparing a contact kit helps to demonstrate your professionalism. It contains a copy of a specimen final report, testimonial letters, brochures, and the like.

Building confidence by doing the little things gives you the extra edge. Confidence builders include reviewing materials ahead of time, ensuring that you present a professional appearance, and getting to the appointment on time.

GUIDING THE MEETING

There are seven parts to conducting a meeting that represents a client-centered new business discussion: opening the meeting; defining a need situation; documenting the existing need situation; outlining the future situation; outlining your proposed solution program; negotiating solution terms; and closing.

Opening the Meeting

Opening the meeting properly helps you to establish a businesslike atmosphere in a friendly way and begin developing a relationship based on trust, confidence, and mutual understanding. This requires:

Managing the introductions. Make your greeting friendly, mentioning the other party's name(s), your name, and your appreciation at being afforded the opportunity to meet with the contract. During this time you want to maintain an "up" face and other nonverbal signals that tell the contact, "You're okay with me."

Managing the seating arrangements. Avoid sitting in an "us and them" fashion such as sitting across a desk from one another. It is quite different and more effective to sit side by side or around a table with the prospect's and your people in a *mixed* seating arrangement.

Bridging to the next phase. After you have chatted enough to reduce the tension that is a normal part of meeting a new client, you simply move on by saying, "I've been looking forward to this opportunity to discuss (mention the need situation)."

Defining a Need Situation

Defining the need lets everyone know that regardless of the outcome of this meeting, it was, in fact, a good idea to meet. The situation you convey, of course, is one requiring your type of resources and experience, and one that is important enough to the contact to invest the time to explore the dynamics, costs, and consequences of the existing situation. You can photocopy Figure 28–1 and take it with you on all selling contacts.

Documenting the Existing Need Situation

This is something that the too-eager service provider often skips. Verify or determine the nature of the need, and define the scope of the need situation. *Who* and *what* is involved? Then determine the contact's costs to date—this will give you a good indication as to the level of the urgency for a solution.

Once you've learned something about the urgency, gently allude to the negative consequences of not proceeding with a solution. Negative consequences include the obvious, such as additional costs, disruption of operations, and low morale, but also, potentially, loss of market share, goodwill, or a leadership position.

Before moving on, take a moment to verify that you and the contact are in sync. If not, review your notes and reframe the scope of work as you understand it; then recheck to see if you and the contact are now in sync.

Outlining the Future Situation

This serves as your bridge in taking the prospect from the theoretical to the actual. In Chapter 1, we mentioned that clients don't buy your

FIGURE 28–1
Interview Guide Questions

1. What is the real need this prospect wants to discuss?
2. What is the scope of the need situation?
3. Where is the need?
   Actually within the organization?
   Felt or observed?
4. When did the situation start?
   When did it become evident?
   To whom?
   How?
5. What has been considered/attempted/accomplished?
   By whom?
   When?
   With what results?
6. Who is this person?
   Title?
   Authority?
   Role in the decision-making unit: influencer, decision maker, initiator?
7. How urgent is the need now?
8. What are the costs and consequences?
   What costs have been incurred to date?
   What are the probable consequences of not proceeding?
9. What is the prospect's solution goal? (How should things be when the need has been solved?)
10. What is the desired/required solutions program?
    Objectives?
    Solution alternatives?
    Work team—who and why?
    Deliverables, in what form and when?
11. Who are the other players?
    What authority does each have?
    What is their stake in the engagement?
    Who will make the actual purchase decision?
    Who will serve as the point of contact?
12. Who will evaluate the results?

service solution; they buy *your promise to produce a more favorable future*. At this juncture, you define the scope of your solution—who will be involved and how. You also determine the contact's timing requirements. When does the project start and when does it need to be completed? To the best of your ability, specify the expected results—the positive conditions to be achieved and the negative effects to be removed or minimized.

Go ahead and make a verbal proposal. You'll undoubtedly speak only in general terms; you'll know more of the nitty-gritty later. Outline or sketch out a solution program that showcases both your approach and your resources, and which confirms that you are the logical solution to the contact's need. This might take the form of a sentence such as, "Let's see what's involved in improving your cash flow by reengineering your accounts receivable process." *Notice that this statement begins with a benefit and reminds the contact of what you are fixing—a truly client-centered approach.*

Outlining Your Proposed Solution Program

Your goal is to suggest an approach that showcases your experience and resources as the logical solution to the contact's need: When outlining the proposed work approach, first discuss the methodology with the prospect. Don't overwhelm the prospect with too many details. The contact wants assurance that you know what you're doing. Focus on the broad tasks and the results you will achieve. Carefully explain the nature and level of assistance that you expect from the prospect and upon which the budget will be predicated; for example, what will the prospect do, how will it be done, and what will the prospect provide?

Next spell out what you won't be doing—what is not part of the engagement. This discussion will reduce misunderstandings further down the road. Mention the proposed budget for the engagement. Try not to discuss fees in specific terms until you are convinced you have an interested and qualified prospect.

Finally, restate the benefits to be received, and then ask, "Am I on target with what you had in mind?" Sit back and listen, because you will automatically move toward agreement on initiating the engagement.

Negotiating Solution Terms

This is a detour you'll likely have to take based on the nature of the prospect's responses. We used to call this overcoming objections. In client-centered marketing, you contemplate the prospect's way of thinking and then attempt to engineer mutual benefits. Regardless of how well you have defined the existing situation and have outlined your proposed solution, there *always* will be concerns, and there *may* be objections to your approach and/or price.

Your goal is to bring to the surface any concerns and objections, calmly acknowledge the prospect's right to have them, and then counterbalance them by restating the benefits, again seeking agreement.

Closing

Closing and satisfying those involved with the purchase decision is your last step *during* the meeting. When you sense agreement regarding your proposed solution, your approach, and the timing, you can move on to closing the deal.

You might say, "To begin improving your cash flow situation, there are few details we need to cover. . . ." If the prospect raises no issues, you launch into the details of getting started on the engagement. If you're not so fortunate, perhaps you'll need to prepare a proposal (see Chapter 29). A proposal details who will be involved from your firm, what office you will work out of, and the like.

End the meeting with a statement confirming the prospect's sound business decision and reemphasizing that you are willing and able to assist the prospect in doing better what the prospect is in business to do. In other words, you specifically reiterate the core solution goal you have mentioned throughout the meeting.

THE POSTMEETING PHASE

The postmeeting phase consists of two main activities: follow-through and evaluation.

Follow-Through

No matter how brilliant you and your team were during the meeting and what level of agreement transpired, you have to keep in mind people often have second thoughts that need to be handled. So, complete actions you promised to take and, if necessary, *resell* the need for your services and the benefits of your solution.

Evaluation

You assess your meeting effectiveness by considering what went well, what was difficult to handle, and whether you formed the basis of a sound relationship with those involved in the meeting. Some firms use a prepared matrix or rating form for self-critique, although all that's really necessary is for you to make some honest notes for the file about the

FIGURE 28–2
World-Class Selling Skills

1. Obtaining an appointment with a receptive existing client or eligible prospective client to discuss a hot-button need situation.

2. Creating an environment in which the prospect feels safe enough to open his "corporate kimono" to you.

3. Using open-ended questions to uncover the current need situation:
   - What's needed, lacking, or not working up to par?
   - What's been done to date, by whom, with what results, costs, and false starts?

4. Defining a need situation specified for the prospect and sketching out your solution recommendation by creating a verbal snapshot of the dynamics, costs, and consequences of the situation.

5. Thinking in the prospect's terms, looking at the business through a more objective lens, and answering the question, "In what demonstrable, financially sound ways can I assist this prospect in doing better what the prospect is in business to do?"

6. Converting the need situation into an improvement goal for which you can deliver a client-centered solution.

7. Working with the prospect, using the prospect's terminology to structure your approach and resources to meet their unique needs.

8. Outlining a solution program that showcases both your approach and your resources as the logical solution to the contact's need.

9. Closing the process early by reminding the prospect of the need to avert the earlier agreed-upon consequences of not proceeding—appealing to the prospect's emotions and as well as intellect.

10. Inducing the prospect to invest resources in your solution program.

11. Taking follow-up action such as preparing a proposal or reselling your solution in the event the prospect has second thoughts.

12. Creating the basis for a continuing relationship through your professionalism and thoroughness, even if this plan is not accepted.

three components cited previously. Jeff frequently pulls out a pocket dictation machine and makes his evaluation minutes after leaving the meeting site. This enables him to recall more vividly what transpired and complete this task quickly.

Figure 28–2 is a handout that Dick uses during his selling skills training workshops. It incorporates elements of this and related chapters in respect to selling a value-adding solution. We suggest that you review this list of selling skills periodically.

CHAPTER 29

Preparing a Winning Proposal

In today's competitive environment it often is customary to prepare a proposal letter that outlines how you intend to produce the results you agreed to during the selling call. The key to writing a successful proposal is to obtain current information on the nature, scope, and needs of the target or a particular solicitation and to present information within the proposal in a manner that convinces the target that hiring your firm represents the best way to accomplish the task.

Entire books and training programs have been written on the subject of proposal writing. The purpose of this chapter is to present the anatomy of a winning proposal.

This chapter will enable you to answer these two fundamental questions:

☐ What are the purposes of a proposal?

☐ What are the sections contained in a winning proposal?

THE PURPOSES OF A PROPOSAL

A proposal has three basic purposes. First, it educates the prospective client about the nature and dynamics of the need situation. Second, it convinces the prospect that you are willing and able to deliver results. Third, it justifies the prospect's investment in terms that are useful and understandable to members of the decision-making unit, the people involved in the selection of the firm.

SECTIONS CONTAINED IN A WINNING PROPOSAL

Introductory Paragraphs

You want to provide introductory comments that are warm, are tailored to the audience, and exude confidence that a mutual understanding will be achieved.

Don't be overly solicitous, using such statements as, "We are grateful for the opportunity to present. . . ." (The prospect is *not* doing you a favor by asking you to prepare a proposal. Indeed, if you do the job correctly, the client is going to derive value from it.)

Some prospects obtain a number of proposals so they can piece them together and try to do the jobs themselves. Our approach stresses results to be obtained, not the specifics on how to go about delivering the results.

The Present Situation

Winning proposals provide a balanced description of the situation. This section is written to avoid embarrassing the reader and to avoid undue criticism from others. Take great pains to positively present the need situation and prior actions. Then you convey your prospect's concerns and interests and how they relate to the present situation.

The Objectives and Scope of the Work

The solution objective, the benefit that will accrue to the prospect, and supporting goals are spelled out in this section. You must also spell out precisely who will do what and what will be included in the solution program.

Our Approach to Solving the Problem

This section discusses what the solution engagement will involve. Winning proposals generally follow this structure:

1. The tasks required to produce the future situation are listed.

2. The products of each task, including the deliverables and intangible factors, such as morale, confidence, and so on, are identified.

3. The benefits statements for each task are fully defined.

Your task is to offer just enough detail to make the prospect appreciate and understand the approach, without committing your firm to an inflexible course of action.

For example, Dick has figured out the process involved in formulating a strategy and positioning a firm in its niche. Instead of giving away the store, he writes, "I will personally work with you and your key people in determining the current and preferred strategic posture for your firm. The posture will contain a definition of the current strategic direction, an analysis of the scope and service mix, and recommendations for using this analysis to position your firm as a leader in the niche."

How We Would Work with You

Surprises are the enemy of good relationships. Your proposal should pinpoint the submission of early and frequent progress reviews. This is especially necessary if the engagement is complex or of long duration. Your goal at all times is to prevent the nagging question, "I wonder what the professional is up to now?"

Give the client credit for having a competent staff with which you can work and communicate well. Offer such statements as, "We will draw upon the experience and creative thinking of your people to build a relationship between your firm and the organization's employees." Keep the prospect's confidence level high.

Anticipated Benefits and End Results

In an eyecatching manner, state in specific terms what you will strive to produce given the resources and time constraints—for example, "As a result of the reorganization of department XYZ, management can expect a substantial improvement in morale and personal performance." Also implicitly justify why the client should hire you, using statements such as, "Using our unique approach" or "We will rely on our 15 years' experience."

Estimate of Time and Charges

You should state the amount that you will charge within a range. If the norms of your profession dictate an alternative way of presenting estimated charges, then use it.

Any reimbursable charges (i.e., out-of-pocket expenses) should be stated separately.

Starting Date

Your availability to start is an important selling point, a fulcrum on which the action proceeds. You need to strike a balance here. If you are available on too short notice, the prospect may wonder why you're not busy. ("No good?") On the other hand, having to wait six to eight weeks can cool off a hot prospect. Even if you are working flat out, you can still find a half day to get the engagement started.

Closing Paragraph

Your closing paragraph should re-emphasize your interest in doing work for this prospective client. "Working with you and your staff to (solution goal) will pay dividends to (name of prospect). We await your approval to proceed."

Qualifications Statement

Depending on how familiar the prospect is with your firm, it may not be necessary to include this section in your proposal.

With this chapter, you have now completed the acquisition process. Next, we'll discuss the myriad of elements included in ensuring client satisfaction.

CHAPTER 30

Ensuring Client Satisfaction

By now, you see that ensuring the satisfaction of all involved in the promotion, purchase, design, and delivery of your value-adding solution can't be left to chance or to halfhearted approaches with too many gaps. Satisfaction results from the gratification and fulfillment of needs and expectations. If anything, you want to make client-centered marketing and ensuring client satisfaction a continuing obsession.

Client expectations are constantly changing, and client requirements of service providers are constantly being ramped up. Your continuing task with clients and prospects is to sense their needs, and sell and install customized services/products that result in satisfaction for all involved. This chapter will show you how to cover the bases.

Upon completing this chapter you will be able to:

☐ Determine the key components of satisfaction expected for your type of business and sought by your type of clients.

☐ Institute a practical satisfaction endurance program in your business.

☐ Feel good about your ability to satisfy clients.

INSIGHTS ABOUT SATISFACTION

Our consulting work with clients worldwide yields several key findings to share with you. First, few clients are satisfied by your value-added factors (i.e., it's what comes out of the solution, not what you put in that truly counts). While you might receive some kudos from clients for your vigorous efforts, they'll retain you long-term only if they perceive great benefit. Their being satisfied with your solution, more than anything, is their state of being. Author and consultant Mack Hanan observes, "Satisfaction cannot be engineered in. . . . It can only be counseled out, trained out, and applied out."

Satisfaction is the result of your ensuring that the expectations of all involved, on the client's end, in the purchase and use of your solution, are met and met *visibly*. This means that you ensure, literally, that the value of your solution is brought to the attention of the appropriate targets. In short, you not only provide a winning solution, you make sure that everyone knows and appreciates its value (however obvious it may be to you and some of the client's people).

If you get nothing else from this book, becoming aware of the need to sell the value of your solution internally, after you've delivered it, will dramatically improve the long-term outlook of your practice.

Satisfaction begins with the way *you* listen and think, and ends with *the client and his people that feel the investment of money, inconvenience, and concern was all worth it.*

A WAY OF LIFE

Ensuring client satisfaction is both a way of life and a core business process for those successful at marketing their consulting and/or professional services. Moreover, ensuring client satisfaction is a mission-critical responsibility with distinct, manageable phases, including:

1. Effective sales processes.

2. Engagement management.

3. Results management.

4. Relationship management.

5. Breakdown-recovery planning.

Effective Sales Processes

During the sales process, the prevailing rule of thumb is to underpromise in the beginning so you can overdeliver at the end. From the outset, you are shaping expectations while you undersell, which is the trademark of the truly client-centered marketing professional. The combination of underpromising and overdelivering requires that you make an accurate and client-centered definition of the current situation and the desired or required future situation.

Engagement Management

Ensuring satisfaction during the engagement requires that you generate high visibility for your assembled work team, especially during the early stages of the engagement. You can accomplish this by holding a first-day lunch with all parties attending, or circulating a memo listing the names and responsibilities of the engagement team in instances where it won't impede their effectiveness. You can also send a small blurb to the editor of the organization's in-house publication or newsletter. When Dick worked with Booz, Allen and Hamilton, the international consulting firm, his mentor taught him the notion of "provident proximity." In plain terms, this means making certain that you are on hand when the client contact is there.

As you proceed toward creating the deliverable, test portions of it with the client's staff members—this keeps your staff visible and keeps more of the client's staff in the loop. An old saying still holds true— "Surprise is the enemy of satisfied clients and repeat business."

Results Management

Results management is a logical extension of engagement management. The core and continuing essence of results management is delivering early, visible results. You don't have to wait until you're well into the project; you can deliver interim or progress reports and summaries of planned activities days after you begin. Such information presented to the right people can pay big dividends. Even seasoned service providers, however, overlook this major opportunity because they get caught up in the day-to-day activities. Too many pros forget that the client wants continual reinforcement that a smart move was made in retaining your firm.

Relationship Management

Effective marketing and selling, as well as ensuring client satisfaction, require the development of sound relationships with the client players. In client-centered marketing, this relationship is a value-based relationship built on trust and sound communications and supported with your insider information and experience.

Some authors refer to this relationship as a win-win relationship. It is characterized by both parties experiencing a win when they have the occasion to interact with each other. Jeff speaks to many groups each year at conventions and conferences. Often, he's asked for a return engagement or to speak to branches or affiliates of the primary group. Jeff makes this happen by thoroughly researching the client, finding out the hot-button needs in advance, and even calling some of the movers and shakers who will be in attendance to get their views on the issues confronting the group.

Then, Jeff arrives the day or evening before the presentation, so that he can meet with the meeting manager and methodically review how to best serve the audience the next day. Both Jeff and the meeting manager feel better for having met beforehand. Afterward, from his perspective, Jeff briefs the manager on what transpired, what worked best, and so forth. Invariably, Jeff and the meeting manager develop a win-win relationship.

Much like Jeff's post-speech briefing, conducting end-of-the-engagement satisfaction meetings is another important step that service providers need to follow. The procedure is simple and powerful. Start by reviewing the nature and details of the assignment(s). This can be in quite a simple form:

> "You wanted . . . ," "we did . . . ," "with the following results. . . ."

Continue by checking the client's perceptions of your assignment:

Did we meet your general expectations?

Where might we have exceeded expectations?

In future engagements, how might we improve our services?

While the iron is hot, introduce your recommendations for additional services by mentioning your policy of bringing needs to the early attention of your client executives. Old-timers refer to this as "planting the seed of need in fertile soil." It's a simple as saying, "You know, we discovered that fewer than half of your engagement contact personnel are using their equipment to optimal capacity. You might want to have us conduct a 'Getting the Most from Your Equipment' workshop for your troops. It's a brief, hard-hitting review of being more effective with less effort. If you like, I'll fax you a copy of the outline, or you can call (mention a client's name) for a reaction to the workshop we held there."

Breakdown-Recovery Planning

Even in the best of situations and relationships, breakdowns occur, schedules are delayed, feelings get hurt, clients don't deliver, and the like. Proactively seeking potential breakdown points is mandatory if you want to ensure satisfaction. While you are planning for the engagement, determine the points where things could possibly go wrong and then

FIGURE 30–1
Recovery Action Sequence

1. Empathize with the client about the consequences and impact. Then, *listen actively to the remarks and tone of voice used by the client.* Your goal is to communicate your concern by your behavior, show that you're willing to hear the client out so you can understand, and convey that you're not interested in arguing. Listen to get the *client's* position, not to score rebuttal points, but to accept what is valid for the client, if not for you.

2. Show urgency in your desire to remedy the situation.

3. Attempt to redress the situation or make amends by giving an unexpected token recompensation if possible. For example, in the event of a problem that he caused, one PC consultant makes amends by providing several hours of training. Hence, he takes visible action to resolve client concerns in ways that are mutually beneficial. No one leaves angry.

4. Follow-up to ensure satisfaction. In real estate, it is said that the three most important factors in a purchase decision are *location, location,* and *location.* In ensuring satisfaction following a service breakdown, the three most important elements are *follow-up, follow-up,* and *follow-up.*

build alert prompts into your routine so that you more quickly head off undesirable events.

If and when things do go wrong, institute the breakdown-recovery process presented in Figure 30–1, moving into action as quickly and professionally as possible.

While this chapter ends, ensuring satisfaction never does for effective service marketers. It is a process that spells the difference between the truly successful and the also-ran.

PART SEVEN

Managing the Client-Centered Marketing Process

CHAPTER 31

Developing Your Strategic Plan

By now, you know well that the client-centered firm adapts its services, promotional strategies, and personal selling approaches to the needs and buying practices of its targets of opportunity. The tools for accomplishing this are the strategic plan and your personal marketing plan.

In this chapter you will learn how to:

☐ Develop your strategic plan.

☐ Define your firm's mission.

☐ Define your purpose.

☐ Articulate the values that underlie your marketing and client service activities.

☐ Make strategic business unit (SBU) decisions.

☐ Allocate your time and resources to appropriate growth strategies.

☐ Prepare your personal marketing plan.

DEFINING YOUR FIRM'S MISSION

A mission statement consists of answers to the following question: "We exist as a firm to do or provide what, for whom, using what technology?"

Here is a mission statement of one successful management consultant: "We are a professional service firm providing written and oral advice and training to clients in the accounting and consulting professions using computer-assisted technology when it delivers value-added results."

DEFINING YOUR FIRM'S PURPOSE

Your purpose statement defines your firm's service commitment to its clients. This is an external focus that spells out what the firm specifically commits to provide to its clients.

Here is an example: "We provide practical solutions in a manner that empowers the client's staff, and produces results far greater than the costs to the client in obtaining the services."

ARTICULATING THE VALUES THAT DRIVE YOUR FIRM

Values refer to the conditions that must be present as you conduct your marketing and client service functions. One of Dick's clients listed the following values:

- Integrity in everything attempted and accomplished.
- State-of-the-art technology—it's enhanced or dropped.
- Client-centered services—promotion and relationship building.
- Strategic focus to avoid dissonant activities.
- Conversion of normative theory into practical choices and actions.

MAKING STRATEGIC BUSINESS UNIT DECISIONS

A strategic business unit refers to the major functional areas of your current practice and the amount of *additional* resources you will devote to each. You can make three decisions: maintain, build, or withdraw resources.

An accounting firm client prepared the table on the opposite page. In this example, it was decided to maintain the current level of resources in the audit side of the practice while investing additional resources in building both the tax and management advisory services functions. No function was to have resources withdrawn from it at this time. The table is simple to prepare, but it requires extensive analysis before making allocation decisions. This process is beyond the scope of this book.

Business	Maintain	Build	Withdraw
a. Audit	X		
b. Tax		40%	
c. Management advisory services		60%	

BUILDING YOUR MIX OF GROWTH STRATEGIES

There are four different strategies for achieving growth: penetration, expansion, innovation, and, in today's rapidly changing environment, retention of one's clients and markets.

1. *Penetration* focuses on increasing sales of current services to existing industry–market niches. This takes several forms:

   a. Sell extensions or add-ons to current engagements.

   b. Sell other services to clients.

   c. Attract new clients within the current niches.

2. *Expansion* concentrates on selling current services to prospects and clients in *new* industry–market niches.

3. *Innovation* focuses on developing and marketing *new services* to targets within both existing niches and new target niches.

4. *Retention* stresses continuation of services to desirable clients you can't afford to lose. Remember that a client saved is a client earned.

The current mix of growth strategies for Dick's practice and for Jeff's practice is as follows:

Growth Strategies for Dick Connor, CMC	
a. Penetration	50%
b. Innovation	20%
c. Expansion	10%
d. Retention	20%

Growth Strategies for Jeff Davidson, CMC

a. Penetration		20%
b. Innovation		30%
c. Expansion		20%
d. Retention		30%

You can include more factors in your strategic plan, but the ones discussed and demonstrated in this section have been proven to be useful to the busy professional.

PREPARING YOUR MARKETING PLAN

You have now been thoroughly immersed in the client-centered marketing approach for the marketing of your professional and consulting services.

It's now time to organize and coordinate those activities that will develop and enhance your relationship with those people who will be interested in using, retaining, or referring your firm and your services. This is most efficiently done by preparing a marketing plan. The charts and work sheets used throughout the book, added to your research efforts and scheduling of client-centered marketing activities, comprise a sound marketing plan.

The rest of the chapter will assist you in preparing your marketing plan and also will provide answers to the following questions:

☐ What are the components of a client-centered marketing plan?

☐ Must some marketing-related thinking occur each day?

☐ Will an effectively implemented client-centered marketing plan work for you?

A CLIENT-CENTERED MARKETING PLAN

A client-centered marketing plan for a professional service firm consists of five components:

1. Assessing one's practice and markets to identify opportunities and problems.

2. Establishing priorities.

3. Setting goals to be accomplished during the marketing planning period.

4. Allocating and organizing the resources required to accomplish the period's goals.

5. Scheduling, applying, and monitoring results.

FIGURE 31–1
Information to Complete Your Personal Marketing Plan

PERSONAL MARKETING PLAN

For:_____

From: __/__/__ to __/__/__
(Current Planning-Action Period)

1. Targets Opportunity
   a. "A" and "B" clients to be contacted this period.
   b. "C" clients with potential for upgrading.
   c. Prospective clients to be contacted.

2. Targets of Attention
   a. "A" and "B" clients with warning signals.
   b. "C" and "D" clients with warning signals.
   c. Referral sources with potential for becoming referral sources.
   d. "A" and "B" clients with potential for becoming referral sources.
   e. Niches requiring attention.

3. Targets of Influence
   a. Potential nonclient influentials to be contacted.

4. Promotion
   a. Promotional actions to be taken this period.

5. Prospecting
   a. Prospecting actions to be taken this period.

6. Other Marketing Actions
   a. Services to be enhanced or developed.
   b. Marketing information systems to be developed.
   c. Self-development actions to be taken this period.

FIGURE 31–2
Sample Form for Your Personal Marketing Plan

PERSONAL MARKETING PLAN

For:_____

From___/___/___ to___/___/___

1. **Targets of Opportunity**

	Who?	*What?*	*When?*
a.	_____	_____	_____
b.	_____	_____	_____
c.	_____	_____	_____
d.	_____	_____	_____
e.	_____	_____	_____

2. **Targets of Attention**

	Who?	*What?*	*When?*
a.	_____	_____	_____
b.	_____	_____	_____
c.	_____	_____	_____
d.	_____	_____	_____
e.	_____	_____	_____

3. **Targets of Influence**

	Who?	*What?*	*When?*
a.	_____	_____	_____
b.	_____	_____	_____
c.	_____	_____	_____
d.	_____	_____	_____
e.	_____	_____	_____

4. Promotion

	What?	Where?	When?
a.	_____	_____	_____
b.	_____	_____	_____
c.	_____	_____	_____
d.	_____	_____	_____
e.	_____	_____	_____

5. Prospecting

	What?	Where?	When?
a.	_____	_____	_____
b.	_____	_____	_____
c.	_____	_____	_____
d.	_____	_____	_____
e.	_____	_____	_____

6. Other Marketing Actions

	What?	Where?	When?
a.	_____	_____	_____
b.	_____	_____	_____
c.	_____	_____	_____
d.	_____	_____	_____
e.	_____	_____	_____

The end product, or hard copy, is the marketing plan. Market planning converts your intentions into commitment and your insights into action. *You must put your plan in writing.*

On completion of a training workshop in setting marketing goals, one firm decided to use their copier to reduce the written plan to pocket size, laminate it, and offer it to staff professionals as a daily memory jogger.

Putting your ideas in writing provides discipline. Hazy thoughts can become precisely formulated strategies when committed to writing. A written plan enables you to measure your progress and to experience a satisfying feeling of accomplishment as you note completion dates for each part of your plan.

We have prepared an extended personal marketing plan form that incorporates figures and recommended marketing steps discussed in the book. Figure 31–1 can be used as a reference in completing Figure 31–2, "Personal Marketing Plan."

SELECT LITTLE GOALS TO WIN EARLY AND OFTEN

To aid in initiating the marketing planning process, sample goals statements are provided in Figure 31–3, a sample financial goals statement in Figure 31–4, and a refresher list of client-centered activities in Figure 31–5.

Build in follow-up. When you set an accomplishment date for a goal, note this in your pocket calendar and desk calendar as a reminder. If you constantly miss goals, determine why. Remember, results accrue over a period of time.

The client-centered marketing approach has proved successful for professional service firms, from some of the very largest to one-person firms. If you effectively implement your client-centered marketing plan, it will work for you.

FIGURE 31–3
Sample Goals Statements

Performance

Financial
Increase average chargeable hour rate from $____ to $____ by __/__/__.
Bill _____ hours in month of ____.
Identify delinquent accounts by __/__/__.

Existing Clients
Identify causes of lost clients by __/__/__.
Contact _____ at _____ to discuss _____ by __/__/__.

Existing Markets
Identify existing markets by __/__/__.
Select one market to estimate potential for growth by __/__/__.

Existing Services
Assess client-centeredness of _____ by __/__/__.
                              (service)
Assess payoff from specialization in _____ by __/__/__.
                                     (industry)

Referrals

Assess the quality of relationship with _____ by __/__/__.
                                        (whom)
Select one referral to "educate" about _____ by __/__/__.
                                       (what)

Targets

Select one prospective client in potential new business pipeline for follow-up
   sales contact by __/__/__.
Identify desirable potential clients in industry _____ by __/__/__.

Promotion

Establish promotion objectives by __/__/__.
Schedule entertainment with _____ by __/__/__.
                            (client)

Other

Attend _____ on __/__/__.
       (program)
Read _____ by __/__/__.
     (publication)

FIGURE 31–4
Financial Goals Statement

For:_____, to (__/___/__)

My financial goals for this period are:_____

_____

_____

_____

_____

I intend to increase my personal billing revenue from_____to
$_____, an increase of___%.
_(most recent 12 months)

I intend to increase the number of personal chargeable hours from ___ to ___,
an increase/decrease of ___%.

I want/intend to increase my average *hourly rate* from $____ to $____.

My key goal to accomplish in this period is:_____

_____

_____

_____

_____

_____

During this planning period I also intend to accomplish the following:_____

_____

_____

_____

_____

The problems I anticipate, if any, in achieving these goals are:_____

_____

_____

_____

_____

The resources I can draw on to help me overcome these problems include:

_____

_____

_____

_____

FIGURE 31–5
Refresher List of Client-Centered Marketing Activities

Existing Key Clients

Retention planning for _____

_____

Expanding services for _____

_____

Referral development with _____

_____

Existing Marginal Clients

Upgrade service and financial relationships with _____

_____

Terminate or transfer _____

_____

Other Existing Client Actions

Corrective actions to remove causes of lost clients _____

_____

Actions to capitalize on sources of desirable new clients _____

_____

Other _____

_____

Markets and Niches

To research _____

_____

To penetrate _____

_____

To abandon _____

_____

Referral Sources

Improve relationships with _____

_____

Develop additional sources—leverage _____

_____

Contact to educate _____

_____

CHAPTER 32

Wrapping It All Up

In marketing your consulting and professional services, from now until your retirement, your responsibility is to sense, sell, serve, and satisfy the needs of your desirable clients, and to continually build upon a client-centered marketing system that you will never outgrow. The key to making it all work for you is to incorporate the strategies and guidelines that form the core of client-centered marketing so that they largely define your regular business procedures. Successful marketing cannot be done on a haphazard basis; it is an integral part of every engagement. This remains true among professionals both aware and unaware of client-centered marketing.

Our experience as consultants and practitioners in the services profession has shown that if client-centered marketing becomes your standard way of doing business, your existing clients will become your private, proprietary market, they're likely to be better served, and your revenue will increase.

At the foundation of all the preceding chapters is the belief that there is no substitute for honesty, integrity, commitment, and an unwavering commitment to delivering quality service.

MAINTAINING YOUR BREATHING SPACE

Chances are, you face many highly challenging tasks, above and beyond that of marketing your services. Realistically, how can you handle it all, be effective, and stay balanced? Here are some of Jeff's observations from his keynote speeches and seminars and from his book *The Complete Idiot's Guide to Managing Your Time* that may help us out of this dilemma.

One hundred years ago, Frederick Taylor and Frank Gilbreth astounded the business world by establishing time-and-motion procedures that enabled employers to get higher productivity from their workers. In doing so, Taylor and Gilbreth established the basis of modern-day time-management techniques, which were widely adopted by executives. But today, time management can no longer solve anyone's problems.

Time management employs rules, such as "handle each piece of paper once." Such rules worked well in a simpler era. When employed today, they lead to major breakdowns.

Roasting the Sacred Cows

The following sacred cows represent conventional time management wisdom. Following each bit of "wisdom" is Jeff's Breathing Space approach that can serve as a guiding principle.

Handling Paper: "Handle each piece of paper once."
Breathing Space perspective: It always depends on what a piece of paper *says*; you may have to handle some papers 25 times, especially if they help you to develop an insider's understanding of your niche! *Never* handle most pieces of paper: don't let them cross your desk.

Reducing Clutter: "When in doubt, throw it out."
Breathing Space perspective: Not bad advice, but hang onto things when you sense downstream consequences of not doing so. Pack up and store current nonessentials and check them again later. Even 10-year-old client notes may have future value, depending on the need situation and how you arrived at the solution.

Being More Efficient: "Speed reading, listening, learning."
Breathing Space perspective: You walk, talk, eat, read, listen, and learn at certain speeds for a reason. Notice that the most successful people in your profession are not in a hurry. It can be harmful for you to accelerate basic personal functioning. As you fully immerse yourself in the needs and opportunities of your clients, you find that speeding through the day can be counterproductive. Operate at a pace that is comfortable for you.

Beating the Competition: "Work smarter, not harder."
Breathing Space perspective: Was Edison smart after some eight thousand attempts to invent the light bulb? When it finally worked,

did his I.Q. rise? Sometimes working longer is warranted. Also, being open to new viewpoints leads to being smarter. We've consistently found that while you may have to work longer in initially assembling your marketing information system, eventually you get to leverage your time and resources. When you can draw upon your keen understanding of your niche and key clients, you'll effortlessly be working smarter.

Managing Your Schedule: "Use sophisticated scheduling tools."
Breathing Space perspective: Electronic calendars, time management software, and so forth will fail when *you* don't keep *them* current. Tackle the few key projects that count; have the guts to leave the rest. Remember you don't employ client-centered marketing with every client and prospect—just the cream of the crop.

Staying Informed: "Read key executive publications."
Breathing Space perspective: More information is generated on earth each day than you could ingest in the rest of your life; it is almost immaterial which and how many publications you read. Choose to keep abreast of broad-based patterns affecting your region, industry, clients, community, or family. Keep abreast of both broad-based patterns and current hot buttons affecting your clients and prospects. You don't necessarily need to do more reading in general; it's likely that you need to do more niche-focused reading.

An Overabundance of Choices

Alvin Toffler predicted in 1970 that you would be overwhelmed by too many items competing for your time and attention. He foresaw that this would inhibit action, result in greater anxiety, and trigger the perception of less freedom and less time. Having choices is a blessing of free market economy. Having too many choices is harmful to your breathing space and results in an increased time expenditure and a mounting form of exhaustion.

Whenever you're about to make a low-level decision either for your firm or for you personally, consider: Does this really make a difference? The service professional today who seeks to stop racing the clock, keep piles from ever starting, and have more energy each day needs new perspectives and fresh approaches for managing career and life. Instead, get in the habit of making *fewer* decisions each day—the ones that count.

The combined effect of facing too much to do each day accelerates the feeling of pressure, although the symptoms are often masked.

If you're too busy to enjoy your life, you're too busy.

If you're too busy to stay calm, you're too busy.

If you're too busy to stay in shape, you're too busy.

On a deeply felt personal level, recognize that, hereafter, you will face an *ever-increasing* array of items competing for your attention, marketing your services always central among them. It is time to make compassionate, though difficult, choices about what is best ignored versus what merits your attention and action.

STARTING TOMORROW

To provide you with quick checklists you can use immediately, we've compiled rosters of "Do's" and "Don'ts," each of which is applicable at *all* stages of the engagement. (See Figures 32–1 through 32–6.) As you put these ideas into practice, you'll begin to realize that your best marketing days are still ahead of you, and that your clients will receive the quality service they are seeking.

FIGURE 32–1
As a Professional, DO

1. Dress in a manner that conveys professionalism and trustworthiness.
2. Maintain a positive attitude toward the client. Communicate your integrity and professional competence in your attitude and behavior.
3. Establish empathy through eye contact and good listening skills. Periodically repeat the client's thoughts to confirm an accurate understanding.
4. Keep abreast of current events and developments in the client's organization.
5. Research the client's industry and market.
6. Be aware of the client's problems and concerns.
7. Return all client phone calls and inquiries promptly.
8. Be punctual for scheduled meetings and appointments.
9. Deliver as promised.

FIGURE 32–2
As a Client-Centered Professional, DON'T

1. Create a relationship of "unequals" with the client.
2. Talk down to the client or offer any antagonistic or patronizing comments.
3. Argue with the client in ways that might hurt self-esteem.
4. Break scheduled appointments or fail to return telephone calls.
5. Offend the client with personal habits, such as smoking if the client doesn't do so.

FIGURE 32–3
In Providing Your Service, DO

1. Obtain a definition of the client's problems and needs in the client's own words.
2. Take a visible interest in the client's business problems.
3. Communicate your expertise diplomatically.
4. Discuss the problem specifics with the client first, not with employees.
5. Estimate the monetary and personal benefits of your service to the client, and make the client aware of those benefits.
6. Inform the client of the availability of other services you provide.
7. Protect the client's self-esteem particularly when discussing sensitive problem areas.
8. Deliver your service on schedule.
9. Maintain regular contact by telephone or in face-to-face conversations.
10. Ensure that the client knows that you are working for the client, and that your efforts are focused on the client's needs and problems.
11. Make your results visible to the client.
12. Copy and mail relevant articles to the client.
13. Get involved in organizations that the client participates in, or share mutual interests.
14. Let the client know that you care about the client as a person, not only as a business colleague.

FIGURE 32–4
In Providing Your Service, DON'T

1. Sell something you don't really want to provide (your heart won't be in it).
2. Undercharge for your services.
3. Ignore or take the client for granted.
4. Let your ego impede developing a relationship of equals, or make the client feel inferior.
5. Make general recommendations or be too vague.

FIGURE 32–5
In Representing Your Firm to the Client, DO

1. Determine what the client wants and needs to know about your firm, and then:
2. Be prepared to explain all of your firm's services in terms of client benefits.
3. Tell the client about your backup personnel.
4. Educate the client as to the competency and reputation of your firm.
5. Make the client aware of your publications and put the client on your mailing list.
6. Inform the client about services your firm has performed for other client.

FIGURE 32–6
In Addressing Client Needs and Problems, DO

1. Identify the problem, what is needed, and what is at risk.
2. Determine the client's future needs.
3. Give the client the opportunity to surface problems.
4. Appraise the client for reactions to your estimated fee.
5. Use tact and be as relaxed as possible.
6. Periodically review the client's position.

Bibliography

Connor, Richard. *Increasing Revenue from Your Clients.* New York: John Wiley & Sons, 1991.

Connor, Richard, and Davidson, Jeff. *Getting New Clients.* New York: John Wiley & Sons, 1994.

Davidson, Jeff. *Breathing Space: Living & Working at a Comfortable Pace in a Sped-Up Society.* New York: MasterMedia, 1991.

———. *The Complete Idiot's Guide to Managing Stress.* New York: Macmillan, 1997.

———. *The Complete Idiot's Guide to Managing Your Time.* New York: Macmillan, 1995.

———. *Marketing on a Shoestring.* New York: John Wiley & Sons, 1994.

Drucker, Dr. Peter. *Management: Tasks, Responsibilities, Practices.* New York: Harper & Row, 1974.

———. *Managing for Results.* New York: Harper & Row, 1964.

Hanan, Mack. *Consultative Selling.* New York: AMACOM, 1995.

McKenna, Regis. *The Regis Touch.* Reading, MA: Addison-Wesley, 1985.

Glossary

AIDA process: creating a favorable awareness (A), sharing information (I) to develop an interest in seeing you, conducting need-driven discussions (D), and building a desire to proceed to action (A).

Client: individual or organization you have served or are now serving.

Client-centered marketing: process that makes an individual client or prospect, in a targeted industry–market niche, the beneficiary of your niche-specific service(s).

Hot-button need: any topic, issue, problem, opportunity, or trend that is of keen interest to the client or prospect whom you are seeking to serve.

Image: mental picture of your firm held by clients and others.

Industry: clients and prospects who are sellers of similar products and services to their customers and prospects (e.g., bankers, hospitals, or manufacturers of tires).

Insider's reputation: favorable awareness of you and your business by clients, prospects, and others who appreciate your niche-specific expertise.

Insider's understanding: in-depth knowledge of the structure and dynamics of the industry and market—how the niche works, what it takes to make a profit and compete successfully, and the key players.

Leveraging: concentrating the smallest amount of your resources on the smallest number of clients, prospects, and other business factors that will produce the largest amount of profitable revenue and results.

Market: industry-specific clients and prospects who are buyers for your services.

Marketing comfort zone: marketing, client service, and new business development activities in which you have confidence, are proactive, and productive in your communications and actions.

Need: hot-button factors the client wants to have handled.

Niche: shorthand for industry–market niche.

Niche influentials (NIs):   opinion leaders and trendsetters who serve, influence, and regulate members of the niche's industry and markets.

Personal selling: face-to-face discussion with a client or prospect regarding a hot-button need.

Promotion: process of informing, persuading, or reminding targets of opportunity and targets of influence about your firm's ability to meet selected needs in the niche.

Prospect: potential client, an organization or individual who has agreed to discuss a hot-button need situation with you.

Prospecting: process of identifying and contacting high-potential "suspect" organizations and individual businesspeople in your markets for appointments to discuss your proposed solution to needs you have reason to believe they have.

Satisfaction: a client's agreement that the solution goals have been achieved.

Strategic alliances: cooperative relationships with other service and product providers serving the niche and with whom you offer complementary resources.

Strategic decisions: "bet-the-farm" decisions involving major resource commitments that determine where and how a business competes against other firms vying for the same clients. Strategic decisions involve focus and concentration of resources, and set the direction of the business.

Suspects: desirable nonclient organizations and individuals possessing suspected needs for your services whom you have yet to contact.

Systems: routine ways of doing things that provide standard results. All systems are processes, but not all processes are systems because some processes can provide variable results.

Targets of attention: important relationships, programs, services, systems, and resources that require corrective action.

Targets of influence: additional niche influentials (NIs) with whom you wish to develop a relationship.

Targets of opportunity: current high-potential clients, prospects, and suspects in your new-business pipeline; all active referral sources, targeted industry–

market niches needing to be cultivated and developed; and potential strategic alliance partners with whom you wish to develop a relationship.

Value: function of a need being met in ways that meet and/or exceed the client's expectations. The client feels that he has earned a suitable return on his investment.

Value-adding solutions: solutions that satisfy the hot-button need, meet or exceed the expectations of those involved in the purchase and use of the solution, and enhance a client's competitive advantage by either lowering cost, increasing revenue, or improving performance/productivity.

APPENDIX A

The Standard Industrial Classification (SIC) Code System

The SIC code system is based on the four-digit Standard Industrial Classification system established by the federal government. This system categorizes businesses into the following broad industry groups represented by the first two digits in the four-digit numeral. The third and fourth digits further identify subgroups within each category.

Agriculture   0100–0999
0100   Agriculture Production—Crops
0200   Agriculture Production—Livestock
       & Animal Specialties
0700   Agriculture Services
0800   Forestry

Mining   1000–1499
1000   Metal Mining
1221   Bituminous Coal & Lignite Surface
       Mining
1311   Crude Petroleum & Natural Gas
1381   Drilling Oil & Gas Wells
1400   Mining, Quarrying of Nonmetallic
       Minerals (No Fuels)

Construction   1500–1799
1520   General Building Contractors—
       Residential Buildings
1540   General Building Contractors—
       Nonresidential Buildings

1600   Heavy Construction Other Than
       Building Const.—Contractors
1623   Water, Sewer, Pipeline, Comm. and
       Power Line Construction

Manufacturing   2000–3999
2000   Food & Kindred Products
2100   Tobacco Products
2200   Textile Mill Products
2273   Carpets and Rugs
2400   Lumber & Wood Products (No
       Furniture)
2451   Mobile Homes
2510   Household Furniture
2520   Office Furniture
2600   Papers & Allied Products
2673   Plastics, Foil & Coated Paper Bags
2711   Newspapers: Publishing or
       Publishing & Printing
2721   Periodicals: Publishing or
       Publishing & Printing

2731 Books: Publishing or Publishing & Printing
2750 Commercial Printing
2800 Chemicals & Allied Products
2911 Petroleum Refining
2950 Asphalt Paving & Roofing Materials
3011 Tires and Inner Tubes
3021 Rubber & Plastics Footwear
3086 Plastics Foam Products
3089 Plastics Products, NEC
3531 Construction Machinery & Equipment
3532 Mining Machinery & Equip. (No Oil & Gas Field Mach. & Equip.)
3533 Oil & Gas Filed Machinery & Equipment
3537 Industrial Trucks, Tractors, Trailers, & Stackers
3540 Metalworking Machinery & Equipment
3570 Computer & Office Equipment
3571 Electronic Computers
3572 Computer Storage Devices
3575 Computer Terminals
3720 Aircraft & Parts
3730 Ship & Boat Building & Repairing
3743 Railroad Equipment
3910 Jewelry, Silverware & Plated Ware
3931 Musical Instruments

Transportation, Communications, & Public Utilities   4000–4999

4011 Railroads, Line—Haul Operating
4013 Railroad Switching & Terminal Establishments
4512 Air Transportation, Scheduled
4513 Air Courier Services
4813 Telephone Communications (No Radio Telephone)
4822 Telegraph & Other Message Communications
4832 Radio Broadcasting Stations
4833 Television Broadcasting Stations
4841 Cable & Other Pay Television Services
4955 Hazardous Waste Management

Wholesale   5000–5199

5000 Wholesale—Durable Goods
5110 Wholesale—Paper and Paper Products
5122 Wholesale—Drugs Proprietaries & Druggists' Sundries

5160 Wholesale—Chemicals & Allied Products
5171 Wholesale—Petroleum Bulk Stations & Terminals
5180 Wholesale—Beer, Wine & Distilled Alcoholic Beverages

Retail Trade   5200–5999

5200 Retail—Building Materials, Hardware, Garden Supply
5211 Retail—Lumber & Other Building Materials Dealers
5531 Retail—Auto & Home Supply Stores
5812 Retail—Eating Places
5900 Retail—Miscellaneous Retail
5912 Retail—Drug Stores and Proprietary Stores

Finance, Insurance & Real Estate Services 6000–6799

6021 National Commercial Banks
6022 State Commercial Banks
6200 Security & Commodity Brokers, Dealers, Exchanges & Services
6211 Security Brokers, Dealers & Flotation Companies
6311 Life Insurance
6321 Accident & Health Insurance
6324 Hospital & Medical Service Plans
6331 Fire, Marine & Casualty Insurance
6500 Real Estate
6510 Real Estate Operators (No Developers) & Lessors
6512 Operators of Nonresidential Buildings
6513 Operators of Apartment Buildings
6798 Real Estate Investment Trusts
6799 Investors

Business & Personal Services   7000–7900

7011 Hotels & Motels
7310 Services—Advertising
7311 Services—Advertising Agencies
7370 Services—Computer Programming, Data Processing, Etc.
7371 Services—Computer Programming Services
7372 Services—Prepackaged Software
7373 Services—Computer Integrated Systems Design
7374 Services—Computer Processing & Data Preparation
7377 Services—Computer Rental & Leasing

7380 Services—Miscellaneous Business Services
7500 Services—Automotive Repair, Services & Parking
7510 Services—Auto Rental & Leasing (No Drivers)
7600 Services—Miscellaneous Repair Services

Health Services   8000–8199

8060 Services—Hospitals
8062 Services—General Medical & Surgical Hospitals, NEC
8071 Services—Medical Laboratories
8082 Services—Home Health Care Services
8090 Services—Misc. Health & Allied Services, NEC
8093 Services—Specialty Outpatient Facilities, NEC
8111 Services—Legal Services

Education & Social Services   8200–8399

8200 Services—Educational Services
8300 Services—Social Services

Art & Membership Orgs.   8400–8699

8400 Services—Museum, Art Galleries, Botanical & Zoo Gardens
8600 Services—Membership Organizations

Engineering, Architecture, & Accounting Services   8700–8799

8711 Services—Engineering Services
8741 Services—Management Services
8742 Services—Management Consulting Services
8744 Services—Facilities Support Management Services

Household & Misc. Services   8800–8999

Government   9100–9799

The best source of up-to-date SIC and business segmentation data can be obtained from American Business Information. Contact them for a free copy of their "Lists of 10 Million Businesses."

American Business Information
5711 South 86th Circle
P.O. Box 27347
Omaha, NE 68127
402-331-7169
http://www.abii.com

A Sampling of Industry, Professional, Small Business, and Trade Associations

ADMINISTRATION, MANAGEMENT

American Management Association
1601 Broadway
New York, NY 10019-7420
(212) 586-8100

American Society for Public
Administration
1120 G Street, NW, Suite 700
Washington, DC 20005-3885
(202) 393-7878

American Society of Association
Executives
1575 I Street, NW
Washington, DC 20005-1168
(202) 626-2723

Data Processing Management
Association
505 Busse Highway
Park Ridge, IL 60068
(312) 693-5070

National Management Association
2210 Arbor Boulevard
Dayton, OH 45439
(513) 294-0421

Sales & Marketing Executives
International
Statler Office Tower, Suite 458
Cleveland, OH 44115
(216) 771-6650

COMMUNICATIONS, GRAPHICS, AND PRINTING

American Association of
Advertising Agencies
Chrysler Building
405 Lexington Avenue
New York, NY 10174-1801
(212) 682-2500

Direct Marketing Association
1120 Avenue of the Americas
New York, NY 10036-8096
(212) 768-7277

International Association of Business
   Communicators
1 Hallidie Plaza, #600
San Francisco, CA 94102-2818
(415) 433-3400

Printing Industries of America
100 Daingerfield Road
Alexandria, VA 22314
(703) 519-8100

Professional Photographers of
   America
57 Forsyth Street NW, Suite 1600
Atlanta, GA 30303-2206
(404) 522-8600

Public Relations Society of
   America
33 Irving Place, 3rd Floor
New York, NY 10003-2376
(212) 995-2230

CONSTRUCTION, CONTRACTING

Air Conditioning Contractors of
   America
1712 New Hampshire Avenue, NW
Washington, DC 20009
(202) 483-9370

Associated Builders and Contractors
1300 North 17 Street, 8th Floor
Rosslyn, VA 22209
(703) 812-2000

Associated General Contractors of America
1957 E Street, NW
Washington, DC 20006-5199
(202) 393-2040

National Association of Home Builders
1201 15th Street, NW
Washington, DC 20005
(202) 822-0200

National Electrical Contractors
   Association
3 Bethesda Metro Center, Suite 1100
Bethesda, MD 20814-3299
(301) 657-3110

Painting and Decorating
   Contractors of America
3913 Old Lee Hwy., Suite 33B
Fairfax, VA 22030
(703) 359-0826

FINANCIAL, REAL ESTATE

American Bankers Association
1120 Connecticut Avenue, NW
Washington, DC 20036
(202) 663-5000

American Institute of Real Estate
   Appraisers
430 North Michigan Avenue
Chicago, IL 60611
(312) 329-8559

American Society of Appraisers
555 Herndon Pkwy., Suite 125
Herndon, VA 20170
(703) 478-2228

American Society of Professional Estimators
11141 Georgia Avenue
Suite 412
Wheaton, MD 20902
(301) 929-8848

Building Owners and Managers
   Association International
1201 New York Avenue, NW, Suite 300
Washington, DC 20005
(202) 408-2662

Financial Executives Institute
10 Madison Avenue
P.O. Box 1938
Morristown, NJ 07962-1938
(201) 898-4600

Independent Insurance Agents of America
127 S. Peyton Street
Alexandria, VA 22314-2803
(703) 683-4422

Institute of Certified Financial
    Planners
3801 E. Florida Avenue
Suite 708
Denver, CO 80210-2571
(303) 759-4900

Million Dollar Round Table
325 W. Touhy Avenue
Park Ridge, IL 60068-4265
(847) 692-6378

Mortgage Bankers Association of
    America
1125 15th Street, NW
Washington, DC 20005
(202) 861-6500

National Association of Bank
    Women
500 North Michigan Avenue
Suite 1400
Chicago, IL 60611
(312) 298-1120

National Association of Professional
    Insurance Agents
400 North Washington Street
Alexandria, VA 22314-9980
(703) 836-9340

National Association of Realtors
430 North Michigan Avenue
Chicago, IL 60611-4087
(312) 329-8200

Security Traders Association
One World Trade Center, Suite 4511
New York, NY 10048
(212) 524-0484

Security Industry Association
635 Slaters Lane
Suite 110
Alexandria, VA 22314
(703) 683-2075

Society of Real Estate Appraisers
225 North Michigan Avenue
Chicago, IL 60601
(312) 819-2400

INTERNATIONAL

Career Women's Forum
Case Postale 39
CH-1211 Geneva 12, Switzerland

Enterprise Development
    Association
High Orchard
125 Markyate Road
Dagenham, Essex Rm 8 ZLB England

Foreign Trade Association
Weyerstrasse 2
D-5000 Cologne 1, Federal Republic of
    Germany

International Association of Crafts & Small
    and Medium Sized Enterprises
Schwarztorstrasse 26
Case Postale 2721
CH-3001 Bern, Switzerland

Intl. Association of State Trading
    Organizations of Developing Countries
Titova 104
Postanski Fah 92
Yu-61000 Ljubljana, Yugoslavia

International Trade Center
Palais des Nations
CH-1211 Geneva 10, Switzerland

World Association of Women
    Entrepreneurs
corso Europa 14
I-20122 Milan, Italy

LEISURE, TOURISM, AND TRAVEL

American Hotel and Motel
    Association
1201 New York Avenue, NW
Suite 600
Washington, DC 20005-3931
(202) 289-3100

American Society of Travel Agents
1101 King Street, Suite 200
Alexandria, VA 22314
(703) 739-2782

National Recreation and Park
    Association
2775 South Quincy Street, Suite 300
Arlington, VA 22206
(703) 820-4940

Travel Industry Association of
    America
1100 New York Avenue, NW
Suite 450
Washington, DC 20005-3934
(202) 408-8422

MANUFACTURING

American Association of Meat
    Processors
P.O. Box 269
Elizabethtown, PA 17022
(717) 367-1168

American Textile Manufacturers
    Institute
1130 Connecticut Avenue, NW, 12th Floor
Washington, DC 20036-3954
(202) 862-0500

Chemical Manufacturers
    Association
1300 Wilson Boulevard
Arlington, VA 22209
(703) 741-5000

Farm Equipment Manufacturers
    Association
1000 Executive Parkway
Suite 100
St. Louis, MO 63141
(314) 878-2304

Industrial Fabrics Association
    International
345 Cedar Building, Suite 800
St. Paul, MN 55101-1088
(612) 222-2508

National Association of
    Manufacturers
1331 Pennsylvania Avenue, NW
Suite 1500, North Tower
Washington, DC 20004-1790
(202) 637-3000

PROFESSIONAL

American Bar Association
750 N. Lake Shore Drive
Chicago, IL 60611-6281
(312) 988-5000

American Institute of Architects
1735 New York Avenue, NW
Washington, DC 20006-5292
(202) 626-7300

American Institute of Certified Public
   Accountants
1211 Avenue of the Americas
New York, NY 10036-8775
(212) 575-6200

American Society of Women
   Accountants
1255 Lynnfield Road, Suite 257
Memphis, TN 38119-7235
(901) 680-0470

Association of Management
   Consultants
230 Park Avenue, #544
New York, NY 10169
(212) 697-9693

Independent Computer Consultants
   Association
11131 South Towne Square
Suite F
St. Louis, MO 63123-7817
(314) 892-1675

Institute of Management
   Consultants
521 5th Avenue, 35th Floor
New York, NY 10175-3598
(212) 697-8262

National Association of
   Accountants
10 Paragon Drive
Montvale, NJ 07645
(201) 573-9000

National Society of Public
   Accountants
1010 North Fairfax Street
Alexandria, VA 22314-1574
(703) 549-6400

Professional Engineers in Private
   Practice
1420 King Street
Alexandria, VA 22314-2794
(703) 684-2862

SMALL BUSINESS

American Business Women's
   Association
9100 Ward Parkway
P.O. Box 8728
Kansas City, MO 64114-0728
(816) 361-6621

American Chamber of Commerce
   Executives
4232 King Street
Alexandria, VA 22302-9950
(703) 998-0072

International Council for Small
   Business
St. Louis University
3674 Lindell Boulevard
St. Louis, MO 63108
(314) 977-3628

National Business League
1511 K Street, NW, Suite 432
Washington, DC 20005
(202) 737-4430

National Federation of Independent
   Business
600 Maryland Avenue, SW, Suite 700
Washington, DC 20024
(202) 554-9000

RETAILING

American Booksellers Association
828 South Broadway
Tarrytown, NY 10591
(914) 591-2665

Food Marketing Institute
800 Connecticut Avenue NW, Suite 500
Washington, DC 20006
(202) 452-8444

Jewelers of America, Inc.
1185 Avenue of the Americas
30th Floor
New York, NY 10036
(212) 768-8777

National Association of Chain Drug
    Stores
413 North Lee Street
P.O. Box 1417-D49
Alexandria,VA 22313-1417
(703) 549-3001

National Association of Convenience
    Stores, Inc.
1605 King Street
Alexandria, VA 22314-2792
(703) 684-3600

National Home Furnishings
    Association
P.O. Box 2396
High Point, NC 27261
(910) 883-1650

National Independent Automobile Dealers
    Association
2521 Brown Boulevard, Suite 100
Arlington, TX 76006-5203
(817) 640-3838

National Restaurant Association
1200 17th Street, NW
Washington, DC 20036-3097
(202) 331-5900

National Retail Federation
Liberty Place
325 7th Street, NW
Suite 1000
Washington, DC 20004-2608
(202) 783-7971

National Retail Hardware
    Association
5822 West 74 Street
Indianapolis, IN 46278-1756
(317) 290-0338

Retailer's Bakery-Deli
    Association
14239 Park Center Drive
Laurel, MD 20707
(301) 725-2149

Shoe Service Institute of
    America
5024-R Campbell Boulevard
Baltimore, MD 21236-5974
(410) 931-8100

WHOLESALING

Durable Goods

American Wholesale Marketers Association
1128 16th Street, NW
Washington, DC 20036-4808
(202) 463-2124

Automotive Warehouse Distibutors
    Association
9140 Ward Parkway, Suite 200
Kansas City, MO 64114
(816) 444-3500

Farm Equipment Wholesalers Association
611 Southgate Avenue
Iowa City, IA 52240
(319) 354-5156

International Wholesale Furniture
    Association
P.O. Box 2482
High Point, NC 27261-2482
(910) 884-1566

National Association of Electrical
Distributors
45 Danbury Road
Wilton, CT 06897
(203) 834-1908

National Association of Wholesaler-
Distributors
1725 K Street, NW, 3rd Floor
Washington, DC 20006
(202) 872-0885

Nondurable Goods

Grain Elevator and Processing Society
Box 15026
Minneapolis, MN 55415-0026
(612) 339-4625

National Tire Dealers and Retreaders
Association
1250 I Street, NW, Suite 400
Washington, DC 20005-3989
(202) 789-2300

North American Building Material
Distributors Association
401 North Michigan Avenue
Chicago, IL 60611-4274
(312) 321-6845

United Fresh Fruit & Vegetable
Association
727 North Washington Street
Alexandria, VA 22314
(703) 836-3410

PUBLIC POLICY

National Governors Association
444 North Capitol Street, NW
Suite 267
Washington, DC 20001-1512
(202) 624-5300

National League of Cities
1301 Pennsylvania Avenue, NW, Suite 550
Washington, DC 20004-1701
(202) 626-3000

State Government Affairs
Council
1255 23rd Street, NW, Suite 850
Washington, DC 20037-1174
(202) 728-0500

U.S. Conference of Mayors
1620 I Street, NW, 4th Floor
Washington, DC 20006
(202) 293-7330

Index

About the Authors

Dick Connor provides consulting assistance for service providers world-wide. He can be reached at:

Dick Connor, CMC
103 Pilot Place
New Bern, NC 28562-8843
Tel.: 1-919-636-1422
Fax: 1-919-636-1021
http://www.connor.net
E-mail: dick@connor.net

For more information on having Jeff Davidson speak at your next convention or meeting, call him at the Breathing Space Institute, or visit the BSI Web site.

Jeff Davidson, MBA, CMC
Breathing Space Institute
2417 Honeysuckle Road #2A
Chapel Hill, NC 27514-6819
Tel.: 1-919-932-1996
Fax: 1-919-932-9982
http://www.BreathingSpace.com
E-mail: jeff@BreathingSpace.com